The Calling

33 1/3 Global

33 1/3 Global, a series related to but independent from **33 1/3**, takes the format of the original series of short, music-based books and brings the focus to music throughout the world. With initial volumes focusing on Japanese and Brazilian music, the series will also include volumes on the popular music of Australia/Oceania, Europe, Africa, the Middle East, and more.

33 1/3 Japan

Series Editor: Noriko Manabe
Spanning a range of artists and genres – from the 1970s rock of Happy End to technopop band Yellow Magic Orchestra, the Shibuya-kei of Cornelius, classic anime series *Cowboy Bebop,* J-Pop/EDM hybrid Perfume, and vocaloid star Hatsune Miku – 33 1/3 Japan is a series devoted to in-depth examination of Japanese popular music of the twentieth and twenty-first centuries.

Published Titles:
Supercell's *Supercell* by Keisuke Yamada
AKB48 by Patrick W. Galbraith and Jason G. Karlin
Yoko Kanno's *Cowboy Bebop Soundtrack* by Rose Bridges
Perfume's *Game* by Patrick St. Michel
Cornelius's *Fantasma* by Martin Roberts
Joe Hisaishi's *My Neighbor Totoro: Soundtrack* by Kunio Hara
Shonen Knife's *Happy Hour* by Brooke McCorkle
Nenes' *Koza Dabasa* by Henry Johnson
Yuming's *The 14th Moon* by Lasse Lehtonen

Forthcoming Titles:
Yellow Magic Orchestra's *Yellow Magic Orchestra* by Toshiyuki Ohwada
Kohaku utagassen: The Red and White Song Contest by Shelley Brunt

33 1/3 Brazil

Series Editor: Jason Stanyek
Covering the genres of samba, tropicália, rock, hip hop, forró, bossa nova, heavy metal and funk, among others, 33 1/3 Brazil is a series

devoted to in-depth examination of the most important Brazilian albums of the twentieth and twenty-first centuries.

Published Titles:
Caetano Veloso's *A Foreign Sound* by Barbara Browning
Tim Maia's *Tim Maia Racional Vols. 1 &2* by Allen Thayer
João Gilberto and Stan Getz's *Getz/Gilberto* by Brian McCann
Gilberto Gil's *Refazenda* by Marc A. Hertzman
Dona Ivone Lara's *Sorriso Negro* by Mila Burns
Milton Nascimento and Lô Borges's *The Corner Club* by Jonathon Grasse
Racionais MCs' *Sobrevivendo no Inferno* by Derek Pardue
Naná Vasconcelos's *Saudades* by Daniel B. Sharp
Chico Buarque's First *Chico Buarque* by Charles A. Perrone

Forthcoming titles:
Jorge Ben Jor's *África Brasil* by Frederick J. Moehn

33 1/3 Europe

Series Editor: Fabian Holt
Spanning a range of artists and genres, 33 1/3 Europe offers engaging accounts of popular and culturally significant albums of Continental Europe and the North Atlantic from the twentieth and twenty-first centuries.

Published Titles:
Darkthrone's *A Blaze in the Northern Sky* by Ross Hagen
Ivo Papazov's *Balkanology* by Carol Silverman
Heiner Müller and Heiner Goebbels's *Wolokolamsker Chaussee* by Philip V. Bohlman
Modeselektor's *Happy Birthday!* by Sean Nye
Mercyful Fate's *Don't Break the Oath* by Henrik Marstal
Bea Playa's *I'll Be Your Plaything* by Anna Szemere and András Rónai
Various Artists' *DJs do Guetto* by Richard Elliott
Czesław Niemen's *Niemen Enigmatic* by Ewa Mazierska and Mariusz Gradowski
Massada's *Astaganaga* by Lutgard Mutsaers

Los Rodriguez's *Sin Documentos* by Fernán del Val and Héctor Fouce
Édith Piaf's *Récital 1961* by David Looseley
Nuovo Canzoniere Italiano's *Bella Ciao* by Jacopo Tomatis
Iannis Xenakis's *Persepolis* by Aram Yardumian
Vopli Vidopliassova's *Tantsi* by Maria Sonevytsky
Amália Rodrigues's *Amália at the Olympia* by Lila Ellen Gray
Forthcoming Titles:
Ardit Gjebrea's *Projekt Jon* by Nicholas Tochka
J.M.K.E.'s *To the Cold Land* by Brigitta Davidjants
Taco Hemingway's *Jarmark* by Kamila Rymajdo

33 1/3 Oceania

Series Editors: Jon Stratton (senior editor) and Jon Dale (specializing in books on albums from Aotearoa/New Zealand)

Spanning a range of artists and genres from Australian Indigenous artists to Maori and Pasifika artists, from Aotearoa/New Zealand noise music to Australian rock, and including music from Papua and other Pacific islands, 33 1/3 Oceania offers exciting accounts of albums that illustrate the wide range of music made in the Oceania region.

Published Titles:
John Farnham's *Whispering Jack* by Graeme Turner
The Church's *Starfish* by Chris Gibson
Regurgitator's *Unit* by Lachlan Goold and Lauren Istvandity
Kylie Minogue's *Kylie* by Adrian Renzo and Liz Giuffre
Alastair Riddell's *Space Waltz* by Ian Chapman
Hunters & Collectors's *Human Frailty* by Jon Stratton
The Front Lawn's *Songs from the Front Lawn* by Matthew Bannister
Bic Runga's *Drive* by Henry Johnson
The Dead C's *Clyma est mort* by Darren Jorgensen
Hilltop Hoods' *The Calling* by Dianne Rodger
Forthcoming Titles:
Ed Kuepper's *Honey Steel's Gold* by John Encarnacao
Chain's *Toward the Blues* by Peter Beilharz
Screamfeeder's *Kitten Licks* by Ben Green and Ian Rogers
Luke Rowell's *Buy Now* by Michael Brown

The Calling

Dianne Rodger

Series Editors: Jon Stratton, UniSA Creative, University of South Australia, and Jon Dale, University of Melbourne, Australia

BLOOMSBURY ACADEMIC
NEW YORK • LONDON • OXFORD • NEW DELHI • SYDNEY

BLOOMSBURY ACADEMIC
Bloomsbury Publishing Inc
1385 Broadway, New York, NY 10018, USA
50 Bedford Square, London, WC1B 3DP, UK
29 Earlsfort Terrace, Dublin 2, Ireland

BLOOMSBURY, BLOOMSBURY ACADEMIC and the Diana logo are
trademarks of Bloomsbury Publishing Plc

First published in the United States of America 2023

Copyright © Dianne Rodger, 2023

For legal purposes the Acknowledgements on p. ix constitute an
extension of this copyright page.

Cover image: Emilija Manevska / Getty Images

All rights reserved. No part of this publication may be reproduced or
transmitted in any form or by any means, electronic or
mechanical, including photocopying, recording, or any information storage
or retrieval system, without prior permission in
writing from the publishers.

Bloomsbury Publishing Inc does not have any control over, or
responsibility for, any third-party websites referred to or in this book. All
internet addresses given in this book were correct at the time of going
to press. The author and publisher regret any inconvenience caused if
addresses have changed or sites have ceased to exist, but can accept no
responsibility for any such changes.

Whilst every effort has been made to locate copyright holders
the publishers would be grateful to hear from any person(s)
not here acknowledged.

Library of Congress Cataloging-in-Publication Data
Names: Rodger, Dianne, author.
Title: The calling / Dianne Rodger.
Description: [1st.] | New York : Bloomsbury Academic, 2023. |
Series: 33 1/3 Oceania | Includes bibliographical
references and index. |
Summary: "Examines the Hilltop Hoods' The Calling (2003), analysing the
album, its impact on Australian Hip-Hop and the sociocultural context from
which it emerged"– Provided by publisher.
Identifiers: LCCN 2022059000 (print) | LCCN 2022059001 (ebook) |
ISBN 9781501392665 (hardback) | ISBN 9781501392672 (paperback) |
ISBN 9781501392689 (ebook) | ISBN 9781501392696 (pdf) |
ISBN 9781501392702 (ebook other)
Subjects: LCSH: Hilltop Hoods (Musical group). Calling. | Rap (Music)–
Australia–History and criticism. | Popular music–Australia–2001-2010–
History and criticism.
Classification: LCC ML421.H536 R64 2022 (print) | LCC ML421.H536
(ebook) | DDC 782.421649092/2–dc23/eng/20221209
LC record available at https://lccn.loc.gov/2022059000
LC ebook record available at https://lccn.loc.gov/2022059001

ISBN:	HB:	978-1-5013-9266-5
	PB:	978-1-5013-9267-2
	ePDF:	978-1-5013-9269-6
	eBook:	978-1-5013-9268-9

Typeset by Integra Software Services Pvt. Ltd.

Series: 33 1/3 Oceania

To find out more about our authors and books visit www.bloomsbury.com
and sign up for our newsletters.

Contents

Acknowledgement of Country viii
Acknowledgements ix
Preface x

1 **Introduction** 1

2 **Origin stories: Hip-Hop in Australia and the Hilltop Hoods' biography** 11

3 **Hip-Hop devotion: 'Testimonial Year' and 'The Calling'** 25

4 **Punchlines and funky beats – 'Dumb Enough?' and 'The Nosebleed Section'** 35

5 **Rocking the party: Live performances** 45

6 **Underground politics – 'Walk On' and 'Illusionary Lines'** 55

7 **Posse tracks and battle raps – 'The Certificate'** 69

8 **Conclusion – 'The Sentinel'** 85

References 103
Index 118

Acknowledgement of Country

I acknowledge the Kaurna peoples, the traditional owners of the land on which I live and work. I pay my respects to their Elders past and present and to all Aboriginal and Torres Strait Islander[1] peoples who are traditional owners of Country throughout Australia. Always was, always will be.

---

[1] In this book, I use the terms 'First Nations' and 'Aboriginal and Torres Strait Islander' peoples interchangeably, noting that there is no agreed collective term for the First peoples of this settler-colonial nation. Other terms appear in direct quotes or in sections where I am employing the language used by the author/s or organization that I am discussing.

Acknowledgements

First and foremost, my immense gratitude to all the passionate people who love, create and promote Hip-Hop culture. Sincere individual thanks to:

- Everyone who gave up their time to participate in interviews for this book and the broader Hip-Hop Histories in Australia project. I really appreciate your willingness to share memories and life-stories with me. It has been a privilege to learn more about your connections to Hip-Hop.

- The University of Adelaide for providing a supportive hub for this research and my teaching, especially, colleagues who mentor and inspire.

- Professor Jon Stratton and the Bloomsbury team for encouraging and constructive editorial guidance.

- John Liddle for meticulous indexing services.

- The extended Rodger and Maud families for all your love, special mention of Gwen Rodger for all your help on the ground in Adelaide.

Adam, Curtis and Nathan – this is for you and because of you.

Preface

This book was written in mid-2022 and includes references to events that were happening at this time. When you are reading this in 2023, it will be the twenty-year anniversary of *The Calling* (2003). This will likely be a time of celebration, nostalgia and critical reflection for Hip-Hop artists and fans. No doubt, there will be new developments that I cannot incorporate into this book. Nonetheless, I hope that my account of *The Calling* contributes to this period of re-assessment, as people both look back on the past and think about the futures of Hip-Hop in Australia.

1 Introduction

Everybody knows the Hilltop Hoods, they're national icons [...]
they kind of helped turn an amateur industry into a cottage
industry into a professional industry. They played a really big
role in that.

(Mark Pollard)[1]

In October 2003, Adelaide Hip-Hop group the Hilltop Hoods launched their album *The Calling* (2003) to a riotous reception at Planet nightclub (*The Advertiser* 2003: 63).[2] The group, comprised of MCs Suffa and Pressure and DJ Debris, had been making music together for over ten years and had built a solid following in their hometown. More broadly, they had earned a reputation as one of the premier groups in the expanding Australian Hip-Hop scene. Based on this following, the Hilltop Hoods had modest expectations for *The Calling*, hoping to sell around 3,000 copies (McMenemy 2006: 50). This would have tripled the success of their previous outing *Left Foot, Right Foot* (2001), which sold 1,000 copies across three weeks of national touring (Duffy 2001: 34). Exceeding all expectations, by 2006 *The Calling* had become the first Australian Hip-Hop

---

[1] Throughout this book I draw on original interviews that I conducted in 2022. A list of participants is provided later in the introduction.

[2] The album launch was held on Saturday the 4th of October in the Adelaide CBD. Adelaide is the capital of South Australia, population 1,781,516 (Census QuickStats 2021). See this 'throwback' post from the Hilltop Hoods Instagram account for photographs: https://www.instagram.com/p/BusEEZwH7cD/.

album to sell 70,000 units which is Platinum status on the Australian Recording Industry Association (ARIA) charts. The album ignited the Hilltop Hoods music career, making them a symbol of the shifting acceptability of Hip-Hop in a 'once rock-dominated society' (Laccarino 2004: 24).

This book explores the success of *The Calling*, a musical release that was so significant that people now use it to explain two distinct periods in Australian Hip-Hop – 'there is before Christ [B.C.] and after Christ [A.C.], right? So, there was before *The Calling*, and after *The Calling*' (Beats). As this quote suggests, the success of the album had significant ramifications for both the Hilltop Hoods and other underground Hip-Hop artists in Australia. While *The Calling* was the Hoods' third full-length album, it was their first release through Melbourne-based Hip-Hop store and independent label, Obese Records. When Obese closed in 2016, owner and Hip-Hop artist Pegz aptly described Obese as 'the little record store that launched Australian Hip-Hop to the masses' (Obese Records Closing Down 2016). The success of Obese and the Hilltop Hoods had 'put everyone on notice that Australian hip hop was now more than just an underground interest' (Double J 2017).

This movement into the national 'mainstream' can in part be attributed to the popularity of two tracks from the album, 'The Nosebleed Section' and 'Dumb Enough?', which received significant radio airplay and charted at number nine and forty-four in the 2003 triple j radio station 'Hottest 100'.[3] When doing promotion for their follow-up album *The Hard Road* (2006), Suffa talked about the new opportunities that had emerged for Hip-Hop artists after *The Calling*: 'there's definitely more media

---

[3]　triple j is a government-funded national youth / alternative radio broadcaster. The Hottest 100 is determined by listener votes.

acceptance, more radio play, bigger shows, more internationals coming through, more promoters, more labels signing Aussie acts – yeah, a lot has changed' (Young 2006: 27). *The Hard Road* reached Platinum status, a sales figure that all the Hoods' albums released since 2007 have achieved or exceeded. The group have been able to maintain their popularity in Australia through a series of changes like leaving Obese and launching their own record label, Golden Era (2008–17) (Hilltop Hoods Newsletter 2008; @HilltopHoods Instagram 2017), and facing new challenges posed by the streaming revolution. As of 2019 they had sold one million albums domestically (Tuskan 2019). In 2020 they announced that they were the most streamed Australian artist on Spotify for the second year in a row with 138.9 million streams (@HilltopHoods Facebook 2020). These are significant feats for artists who are from a country where the adoption of Hip-Hop was dismissed as 'cringe worthy' for years.

For decades, 'Australian Hip-Hop' was seen as an example of a foreign cultural form usurping local culture – an emblem of the dire impacts of globalization.[4] This narrative was supported by the adoption of American accents by many artists in the 1980s and 1990s, a practice that was common until rapping in a local accent became normalized. I explore these issues in more detail in Chapter 2 where I problematize categories like 'local',

---

[4] As I discuss later in the Introduction, these issues have been less prevalent for First Nations artists and fans who may not identify as 'Australian'. This is because Australia is a settler-society created through the violent 'dispossession of the original owners of the land' (Moreton-Robinson 2015: 5). For this reason, while I use the term 'Australia' in this book I note that I am 'using a colonialist title, and one that has historically obfuscated the Indigenous nations of Australia, for whom sovereignty was never ceded' (Hoad and Gunn 2019: 4).

but for now I want to note that the Hilltop Hoods were staunch supporters of rapping in one's own accent. This position was celebrated locally but undoubtedly created issues for them in international markets. As a reviewer in Canadian magazine *Exclaim!* put it, they 'will most likely only ever have a cult appeal in North America – rap in an Australian accent is just too much for most people to handle' (Dart 2012). This means that while the Hoods have become a respected institution in Australia, they have not achieved significant global success. They have conducted a number of international tours to sell-out audiences; however, attendees are often Australian expatriates or hard-core Hip-Hop practitioners who have heard about them through word-of-mouth and niche media.

The difficulties of achieving success in the United States – the home of Hip-Hop and a dominant cultural centre – have been discussed by the Hoods in interviews and are not unique to them. According to a 2016 Billboard article, 'no hip hop artist from the UK, Australia or New Zealand, rapping in their native accent, has ever charted in the top 20 albums or top 10 singles in the US' (Castigilia 2016). Hip-Hop artists who were born in Australia and have been successful in North America include Iggy Azalea who does not identify with the Australian Hip-Hop scene (Morrisey 2014: 4), and more recently, Kamilaroi rapper The Kid LAROI, who was nineteen at the time of writing and was born in the same year that *The Calling* was released. Although LAROI has been described as a Hip-Hop or Trap artist, his music is eclectic and he does not define his music with a singular label (Glicksman 2021). Iggy Azalea has been criticized for differences between her everyday speech and her lyrical style which incorporates linguistic markers from African American English (Eberhadt and Freeman 2015).

Both the southern US Hip-Hop inspired drawl of Iggy Azalea and the diverse SoundCloud, emo-rap aesthetic of

The Kid LAROI are far removed from *The Calling*, which is heavily inspired by 'boom bap' early 1990s Hip-Hop. The Hoods cite a list of both iconic US pioneers and more contemporary underground acts as influences including Public Enemy, Ice T, Notorious B.I.G., Nas, A Tribe Called Quest, Jurassic 5, the Roots, and Pharoahe Monch (Dullroy 2003: 50; *The Advertiser* 2005; Eliezer 2018). These sonic inspirations are heard in the sample-heavy, funk-based, stripped back production of the album and in the use of other conventions like a 'posse track'. In this book, I trace these connections, examining how the album fits within both international and local contexts. I explore specific tracks from the album that I have grouped together to consider shared themes. Unless otherwise noted, my analysis is based on the 2003 CD version released by Obese Records that has seventeen tracks. This includes the bonus song 'The Sentinel', which was not included on the 2003 Obese Records vinyl version. The vinyl release added another track, 'All On Me feat. Pegz and Layla', and slightly changed the track order. To ensure that my work abides by fair use/fair dealing and does not infringe copyright, I do not quote lengthy sections of lyrics from the album. I strongly encourage people to listen to the songs that I discuss as they read through the chapters.

Analytical approach

In this book, I analyse the album itself, the Hilltop Hoods' career/live performances, and the broader socio-cultural context that shaped how *The Calling* was produced and received. I use the album as a lens to critically reflect on the beliefs and practices of Hip-Hop enthusiasts in Australia, including changes over time. Overall, the book seeks to document the immediate and long-term impact of *The Calling* and to contribute to a growing number of studies that explore the histories of Hip-Hop in Australia. Although I have interviewed people from across the country, this history is Adelaide-centric and focuses on the mid-2000s period. My approach is informed by my research background as a socio-cultural anthropologist, an orientation which means that I commit the cardinal sin of any book about music – prioritizing discussion of cultural beliefs, ideologies, histories and lyrical messages above consideration of the music itself. I have been a Hip-Hop fan since my early teens and began researching Hip-Hop in 2006 for my PhD in anthropology.

I conducted an ethnographic study of the Adelaide and Melbourne Hip-Hop scenes based on fieldwork from 2006 to 2008. This research explored how Hip-Hop was being localized in Australia, including how Hip-Hop artists and fans were constructing and performing 'authenticity'. I conducted this project after the Hilltop Hoods had broken into the mainstream and they did not respond to an interview request in 2007. Nonetheless, I found that their presence was ubiquitous. They were frequently mentioned in interviews that I conducted with other Hip-Hop artists and fans. I also attended several of their performances that I documented in fieldnotes. Here I want to acknowledge my positionality as both an academic who writes about Hip-Hop in Australia and a Hip-Hop fan. This means that my interest in the Hoods is both personal and professional. In my account of *The Calling*, I try to leverage these positions by combining my own subjective analysis with information from a range of media resources and primary research.

Unfortunately, both the Hilltop Hoods and Pegz declined interview requests for the present project. To address this gap and draw in first-hand accounts from them and other Hip-Hop artists, I use media interviews from newspapers, street press and Hip-Hop magazines that I have collected or accessed digitally. I also conducted semi-structured interviews with fifteen Hip-Hop artists/media professionals from across Australia.[5] I recruited participants through direct approach using publicly available contact details and via social media calls. Six interviews solely focused on *The Calling* and went for twenty-eight minutes to one hour. The remaining interviews were broader and formed part of a larger project exploring the histories of Hip-Hop in Australia with one section about *The Calling*. These interviews typically ran for one to two hours. Four interviews were conducted via email and eleven were video meetings or telephone calls that were recorded and transcribed. Twelve participants identified as male and three identified as female. Because I primarily approached Hip-Hop practitioners who were active when *The Calling* was released, the average age of participants was forty-two. Future work could consider how the album and the Hoods are understood by younger artists and fans.

List of interview participants

Here I give some brief information about each interview participant to help contextualize quotes that are woven throughout the text. I list them in alphabetical order and have included their location when *The Calling* was released.

- Anthony Lewps/Lewps 264: Member of the Cypher Crew, radio host, promoter, creator and editor *Illegal Fame Magazine* – Adelaide.

---

[5] Research activities were approved by the Human Research Ethics Committee at the University of Adelaide (H-2022-026).

- Ben Funnell: Creative Director at April77 Creative, graphic designer for numerous Hip-Hop artists including the Hilltop Hoods – Sydney/Canberra.

- Beats: Producer/MC, solo artist, member of Adroit Effusive and host of the podcast 'The Get Down' – Adelaide.

- Ben Iota or Bornski: Producer/MC, solo artist, member of groups Adroit Effusive and Common Cause, creator of archived music interview website 'BEAT CONTEXT' – Adelaide.

- Chris Bass[6]: Producer/MC, Bass player, solo artist and member of multiple Hip-Hop and funk/jazz groups including 9th Circle, Hooded Puppets, Capital F, Bliss, and Defenders – Adelaide.

- Dazastah: Producer/MC, member of Downsyde and Syllabolix Crew,[7] Hip-Hop workshop facilitator – Perth.

- DJ Sanchez: DJ/Turntablist, Hip-Hop and RnB promoter, host of The Lesson 92.7 – Adelaide.

- DJ Josie Styles: DJ, radio host, journalist, employee Next Level Records, publicist Shogun Entertainment – Sydney.

- Kultar Ahluwalia: Producer/MC, Koolta, Daydream Fever, We Move Like Giants, Hip-Hop workshop facilitator – Adelaide.

- Layla: MC, member Syllabolix Crew – Perth.

- Mark Pollard: Editor of Hip-Hop magazine *Stealth*, radio host, journalist – Sydney.

---

[6] Chris Bass is Matt Lambert's (Suffa's) older brother. He is one of four boys in the Lambert family. He is featured on two tracks on the Hilltop Hoods' EP *Back Once Again* (1997) with the group Hooded Puppets. He also played bass on other Hilltop Hoods' releases including *The Hard Road* (2006).

[7] Syllabolix (SBX) is a Perth Hip-Hop collective.

- Maya Jupiter: MC, solo artist and member of Foreign Heights, producer and host of the triple j Hip-Hop Show (2004–8), Channel [V] host of Soul Kitchen and Freestyle Countdown (2003–9) – Sydney.

- MITUS: MC/producer and promoter – Newcastle.

- Raph AL: MC, member of Certified Wise, Terra Firma – Adelaide/Melbourne.

- Tomahawk: MC, member of Clandestien and Syllabolix Crew, artist – Perth.

As seen at the beginning of this chapter, many sections of the book open with a pertinent italicized quote that relates to the content.

Chapter overviews

In Chapter 2, I provide a brief overview of the histories of Hip-Hop in North America and Australia before discussing the formation of Obese Records and the Hilltop Hoods' career to date. Chapter 3 argues that the most prominent message on the album is the group's love, passion and commitment to Hip-Hop. Chapter 4 explores the Hoods' lyrics and song structure through an analysis of 'Dumb Enough?' and 'The Nosebleed Section', leading into a discussion of their prowess as live performers in Chapter 5. Chapter 6 looks at the introspective and political tracks, 'Walk On' and 'Illusionary Lines', and considers the importance placed on being independent during this era. Chapter 7 examines how a battle rap/competitive ethos shaped the album. The final chapter uses the track 'The Sentinel' as a starting point to think about the legacy of *The*

Calling. The influence of the album is perhaps best summed up by Yorta Yorta MC Briggs who said that 'even if you weren't a fan of the Hilltop Hoods, you couldn't deny that this was the icebreaker' (Double J 2017). This book explores why this album 'broke the ice' and the ramifications this had for a rapidly growing Australian Hip-Hop scene.

2 Origin stories: Hip-Hop in Australia and the Hilltop Hoods' biography

I remember back in the day going to play with the Hoods with thirty people watching us. All of a sudden, like fuck, they're filling stadiums. [...] you really get to see the impact that us young hoodlums had on the scene. It's crazy.

(Raph AL)

In the important book *Black Noise* (1994: 2) Tricia Rose describes Hip-Hop as an 'African-American and Afro-Caribbean youth culture composed of graffiti, breakdancing and rap music', components that are now more commonly referred to as the 'Four Elements' of Hip-Hop: MCing, DJing, Graffiti Writing and Breaking.[1] Her work documents the origins of Hip-Hop in post-industrial New York City in the 1970s, a period when South Bronx neighbourhoods were being destroyed by a series of brutal 'urban renewal' policies that saw large sections of housing razed (1994: 30–1). She writes that against this backdrop, young African American, Jamaican, Puerto Rican and other Caribbean people

---

[1] Throughout this book I capitalize the word 'Elements' which is used to refer to the Four Elements of Hip-Hop. In the mid-2000s in Australia many people used this term; however, there has always been contestation about how many Elements comprise Hip-Hop culture and their historical and ongoing relationship (Rodger 2019).

created Hip-Hop as an alternative site of 'identity formation and social status in a community whose older local support institutions had been all but demolished along with large sectors of its built environment' (1994: 34).

Since its inception in the Bronx, Hip-Hop scenes have flourished across North America, with specific geographic regions becoming associated with their own distinct traditions. Justin Williams (2015: 5) argues that artists from the East Coast dominated during the 1980s, followed by West Coast artists in the 1990s and Southern artists in the late 1990s. As Hip-Hop expanded and transformed across the United States, it was simultaneously being adopted beyond these roots. From the late 1970s onwards, people around the world, including Australia, learnt about Hip-Hop through interpersonal exchanges and via mass media. To date, a detailed academic account of the histories of Hip-Hop in Australia has not been published but practitioners themselves have always documented and archived Hip-Hop in various formats. This includes radio shows, podcasts, documentaries, magazines, Graffiti book projects, and more recently, social media accounts. My aim here is not to set out a chronological history of Hip-Hop in Australia but to provide a broad sketch of events that shaped the production and reception of *The Calling*.

Most academic scholarship that has been produced about the early development of Hip-Hop in Australia focuses on the 1980s–1990s Sydney scene (see Mitchell 1999; Maxwell 2003), which has been described as a diverse and vibrant community that included women,[2] First Nations artists like Jardwadjali MC

---

[2]   There has been limited discussion of people who identify as non-binary, queer or gender fluid in Hip-Hop scholarship, particularly writing that looks at the early histories of Hip-Hop culture. See also Chapter 7 and the conclusion for further discussion.

Munkimuk (Minestrelli 2016), and people from many different ethnic backgrounds (Fernandes 2011). Media texts that were important in sparking the development of Hip-Hop in Australia included films like *Wild Style* (1983), *Flash Dance* (1983), *Style Wars* (1983) and *Beat Street* (1984); the book *Subway Art* (Cooper and Chalfant 1984) that documented New York Graffiti and the follow up *Spray Can Art* (Chalfant and Prigoff 1987); and music like Malcolm McLaren's 'Buffalo Gals' (1983) (see Maxwell 2003). All Hip-Hop Elements were taken up quickly in Australia but Breaking and Graffiti were particularly popular. Many Hip-Hop practitioners from this era can recount the mind-blowing moment when they first saw the dexterous movements of a Breaker or colourful 'wild style' Graffiti lettering, a revelation that set them on a Hip-Hop journey (D'Souza and Iveson 1999: 58).

As seen in the 'Buffalo Gals' film clip, these Elements were frequently combined into an entire 'package' to which people in Australia were introduced as a combined entity from the mid-80s onwards. Despite this packaging, it took more time for locally produced Hip-Hop music to start emerging, in part because of the hesitancy around using local accents. As Sydney Hip-Hop icon Blaze explained, people were limited by the 'initial feeling that rap would only sound good in an American accent' (D'Souza and Iveson 1999: 58). Similarly, Suffa notes that artists had to fight 'stereotypes and assumptions that the public had about Australian Hip-Hop, trying to break down barriers, the misconception that just because Hip-Hop is an American art form that we can't make it an Australian art form as well' (Young 2006: 27). Yet, *if* and *how* Hip-Hop should be 'made' Australian was a problematic issue for many people because of the 'inherent tensions involved in adapting decidedly Black cultural forms to a white-dominated society' (Kelly and Clapham 2019: 147–8). For white artists and fans, concerns about cultural appropriation, ownership and imitation have been prominent. Groups like the Hilltop Hoods had to work to reject claims that they were trying to be Black or 'wannabe Americans', as seen in this quote from Suffa: 'this is not Australians trying to be American, this is Australians doing hip-hop as Australians' (Young 2006: 27).

In a book chapter titled 'Decolonizing Aussie Hip Hop' that explores Aboriginal Hip-Hop, Kelly and Clapham (2019: 150) demonstrate that these issues have not been as fraught for First Nations artists who often self-identify as Black and have a long history of dialogue and engagement with African diasporic people and cultural forms, including participation in transnational anti-racism movements. Similarly, Tony Mitchell, a popular music scholar who has written several accounts of Hip-Hop in Australia (c.f. Mitchell 1999; 2001; 2003), notes that part of Hip-Hop's attraction for people from culturally and linguistically diverse backgrounds has been the powerful space it provides for both articulating and challenging their 'otherness within Australian society' (Mitchell 2001: 28). In a later chapter, Mitchell (2003: 200) also argues that the rejection of Hip-Hop by the broader Australian public in the late 1990s and early 2000s was shaped by their misconceptions about African American culture and was also a manifestation of 'xenophobia towards non-Anglo migrant youth and Aboriginals'.

During this time frame, the Hip-Hop scene could best be described as an underground, DIY subculture made up of passionate artists and fans who were building their own social networks and expertise. It would be remiss not to mention that many of these networks were created by Graffiti Writers, who kept the culture alive in the late 1980s and early 1990s when mainstream media interest in Breaking had faded. At this time, Hip-Hop music shows were sporadic and attended by small crowds that were often made up of rival Graffiti crews. For example, Pressure describes playing small shows in Adelaide to between 50 and 100 people in 'back rooms and seedy pubs' in 1996 (Wehner 2006: L14). In this context, using a local accent and rapping about culturally specific themes were central ways that artists in Australia emphasized their authenticity. For some, these were also strategies used to distance themselves from criticisms about their legitimacy, ways to highlight their originality and the local relevance of Hip-Hop.

Inspired by UK artists like London Posse and home-grown examples like Def Wish Cast and the AKA Brothers who rapped in their own accents, many Hip-Hop practitioners started to reject people who assumed an American accent when they rapped. It became expected that people would use their 'local' accent in their rhymes and artists who did not were heavily criticized. Of course, this raises an important question, what is a 'local' accent? In the early years of Hip-Hop a 'local' accent could range from an 'Ocker' (white) accent to a 'Polynesian-, Aboriginal-, Filipino-, or Lebanese-Australian accent' (Kelly and Clapham 2019: 149). However, as Hip-Hop became more popular in the 2000s, a broad 'Ocker' accent started to become normalized (O'Hanlon 2006; Kelly and Clapham 2019: 153) and some Hip-Hop artists felt pressured to adopt it. In an exegesis which accompanies his film *JustUS: What Hip-Hop Wants You to Know*, Biripi scholar and MC, Grant Saunders (2020: 81–2) explains that the widespread rejection of American accents resulted in some Indigenous artists and rappers from culturally and linguistically diverse (CALD) communities being excluded from the dominant 'Aussie' Hip-Hop community or choosing not to participate in it.

For example, Gumbaynggirr MC Wire has said that he felt like he was being colonized by white Hip-Hop practitioners who pushed him to use a particular accent, 'having White boys come up to me and saying "You know, maybe you should rap a bit more Aussie." And I'm like "What?! Are you trying to colonise me again dude?! Stop it. Stop it"' (Pennycook and Mitchell 2009: 37). According to MC Raceless from Melbourne Hip-Hop group Curse Ov Dialect,[3] in the mid-2000s 'Aussie Hip-Hop' started to be seen as an 'Anglo thing' and this resulted in 'ethnic rappers trying to be more Anglo' (Rule 2008). In both above quotes, MC Wire and MC Raceless use the phrase 'Aussie'. This is significant because many Hip-Hop practitioners in Australia have mixed feelings about the labels 'Australian Hip-Hop', 'Aussie Hip-Hop' or 'Oz Hip-Hop'. In an interview for this book, Perth MC and artist Tomahawk said that he hated the term 'Australian Hip-Hop' with every midichlorian in my Sith-frame.[4] I make Hip-Hop music. If the rest of the world cannot see us as Hip-Hop, then they are just plain stupid. "Australian Hip-Hop" is straight up disrespectful.'

This was a common viewpoint shared by Hip-Hop practitioners who saw no reason to add a national descriptor in front of the term 'Hip-Hop'. Others thought that the terms 'Aussie' or 'Oz' Hip-Hop could be useful short hands, but were also associated with nationalistic stereotypes and clichés. For this reason, many people avoided them. Chris Bass said he thought the term 'Oz Hip-Hop': 'just reeks of that kind of rapping where, they're rapping about sinking brews and all the clichés

---

[3] Curse Ov Dialect have been described as 'avant-garde, experimental, surrealist and Dadist' (Attfield 2020: 111). Their music includes messages that reflect on 'what it means to be Australian in a multicultural but often racist society' (Attfield 2020).
[4] The terms 'midichlorian' and 'sith' are references to the Star Wars universe created by George Lucas. I interpreted this quote as being equivalent to the saying 'with every fibre of my being'.

[…] I'm an Australian and sunburned country, blah, blah, blah'. At worst, this clichéd patriotism was also connected to broader concerns about white nationalism and racism amongst Hip-Hop fans. As one of the most successful Hip-Hop acts from Australia whose members are generally regarded as 'white', the Hoods are implicated in debates about whether the scene is a monocultural space where racist ideologies are festering, and how this can be addressed. I explore these issues further in the final chapter of this book. First, I want to provide more details about Obese Records and the formation of the Hoods.

Breaking into the mainstream: The success of Obese Records and the Hilltop Hoods

As mentioned in the opening of this book, Obese Records were an independent record label and store based in Melbourne. Their story begins in 1995, when Ollie Bobbitt opened a Skate and Hip-Hop clothing store in Prahran called 'OB's' with a record section. When Bobbitt sold the business to his partner Shaheen Waheed (Shazlek One), it was renamed with the pun 'Obese' (Rap News 2004). The official biography of Obese Records suggests that the label and distribution services were added when new owner Pegz (Tirren Staaf) took over in 2002 (Obese Records Website, Biography n.d.). However, the label was active in 2000 and 2001, a period when Pegz worked at the store but had not yet purchased it (Beat 2010). According to a recent interview on the Hip-Hop podcast 'Beers, Beats & The Biz' (2021), Shazlek One was responsible for early Obese Records' releases including MC Reason's *Solid* (2000), the first

Culture of Kings (2000) compilation discussed below and Brad Strut's *The Authentic* (2001).

Like many record stores across Australia, Obese was a hub for both Hip-Hop locals and inter-state travellers who would head straight for the shop when they visited Melbourne. In Adelaide in the mid-2000s, equivalent social centres were B Sharp, Big Star, Clinic 116 and Da Klinic.[5] I have very fond memories of walking through the first level of the Big Star city store and down the steep wooden staircase to the gloomy lower level that housed Hip-Hop vinyl, documentaries, magazines and other merchandise. I was not a massive record collector but flipping through stacks of vinyl, hunting for a new purchase was immensely satisfying. I was also able to visit the Obese Prahran store in 2007, using it as a base to conduct interviews for my PhD in nearby cafes. At this time the reputation of Obese Records was firmly cemented, having been building steadily since the early 2000s.[6]

Obese was 'fertilising the scene' (Gregson 2004: 18) as Hip-Hop groups were starting to be recognized outside of the tight-knit circle of underground Hip-Hop heads. Perth MC Layla described this as an 'exciting' time when 'people were beginning to get used to the Australian accent in rap music and appreciate the quality and diversity of the work'. Events that contributed to this growing appreciation included the creation of a national Hip-Hop show by the youth broadcaster triple j in 2001,[7] the international popularity of American MC Eminem,

---

[5]   Prior to this a key store was Central Station in Rundle Mall.

[6]   Another important independent record label in this era was the Sydney-based Elefant Tracks.

[7]   This show was not well received by all Hip-Hop fans/artists because it was initially hosted by Nicole Foote who was a dance DJ and existing radio host at triple j who was not connected to the Hip-Hop scene.

and the success of the 2002 track 'Karma' by Melbourne Hip-Hop group 1200 Techniques[8] which won ARIA awards for best video and best independent release. Maya Jupiter said that *The Calling* continued the momentum of mainstream appeal that 1200 Techniques experienced with Karma: 'we're coming, and we're making our own roads, whether you like it or not. We're here. That's what the statement was. We're here to stay.' The creation of these new roads was helped by Obese Records releasing compilation albums – three *Culture of Kings* volumes (2000, 2002 and 2003),[9] and *Obesecity* (2002).[10] These albums brought together artists from across Australia and helped to promote the scene. Melbourne MC Bias B, who worked at the Obese retail store, said that when triple j named *Culture of Kings: Volume Two* (2002) album of the week, Obese started receiving 'a lot of phone calls' (Murphy 2004: 71). This album featured a diverse range of tracks, including the Hilltop Hoods song 'The Sentinel' which also appears on the CD release of *The Calling*.

The expansion of Obese Records and the popularity of *The Calling* were two significant events in the history of Hip-Hop in Australia. It could be argued that their success was intertwined (Pollard 2004a: 8). As Kultar Ahluwalia put it: 'the Hoods blowing up and Obese Records blowing up sort of happened simultaneously'. This mutual relationship was highlighted in the results of a 2003 readers' poll in the Australian Hip-Hop magazine *Stealth* (2004) where the Hilltop Hoods took out 'Best Group' and Obese was awarded 'Best Record Label' with over 70

---

[8] The members of 1200 Techniques are DJ Peril (Jason Foretti), Kemstar (Simon Foretti) and N'Fa Jones.

[9] DJ Dyems from Adelaide Hip-Hop group Terra Firma played a central role in the production of the *Culture of Kings* albums.

[10] Another key compilation prior to this was *Rock Da City* (1999) released by Melbourne label Nuffsaid.

per cent of the votes. When tracks from *The Calling* were picked up by mainstream radio broadcasters, the Hilltop Hoods were able to sell out four consecutive shows at the Corner Hotel, an iconic rock venue in Melbourne. Tellingly, media reports about the show compared the Hoods to Australian rock group Midnight Oil, noting that they had achieved a feat that 'not even Midnight Oil could manage' (Donovan 2004: 4).

By 2004, the Hoods were playing to large audiences, including being a central part of an event titled the Obese Block Party in Melbourne that saw 2,200 people come out to support the label's roster. The popularity of the Hilltop Hoods exposed people to other artists, becoming an entry point into the wider scene. Other acts signed to Obese at this time included Bias B, Bliss n Eso, DJ Bonez, Drapht, Downsyde, Hyjak n Torcha, Layla, Muph n Plutonic and Reason. In the interview extras on *The Calling Live* (2005), these fellow label mates are described by the Hoods as a family and Suffa says that Obese Records played a key role in promoting Hip-Hop culture in Australia. The solid friendships that were formed during this period were commented on by Layla who said that she was still 'good friends' with the Hoods and had 'so much respect for the boys and the SA crew'.

Layla was also signed to Obese who released her debut *Heretik* (2005). She described Obese Records as playing 'a prominent role in the Australian Hip-Hop scene for many years'. The 'huge impact' of Obese and the legacy of Ollie Bobbitt, Shazlek One and Pegz was further highlighted by Anthony Lewps who said that they had 'the biggest roster, extremely professional distribution team as well as the credibility that came with the fact that it was created by the artist for the artists'. According to Lewps, Obese were 'at the forefront for a very long time in regard to artist development and certainly turbocharged Hip-Hop in Australia, opening the door for many artists to be heard'. Lewps signed off by giving 'much respect to Ollie Bobbitt, Shazlek One and of course Pegz!'

Hilltop Hoods' biography

Here it is useful to provide some specific details about the formation of the Hilltop Hoods and their career to date. MCs Suffa (Matthew Lambert) and Pressure (Daniel Smith) met and started rhyming when they were both students at Blackwood High School in Adelaide in the early 1990s. The group's original DJ was DJ Next who was involved in their first demo titled *Highlanders* (1994). This demo also featured MC Summit, later known as DJ Sum-1. Around this time, the group met DJ Debris (Barry Francis) and they 'just clicked' (Suffa in Hegarty 2003: 17), with Debris initially playing a producer and sound engineer role in the group.[11] In 1997, they released their first EP, *Back Once Again*. The follow-up full-length album (*A Matter of Time* 1999) was the last project that included DJ Next as a core member.[12] *Left Foot, Right Foot* (2001) cemented the line-up, Debris, Suffa and Pressure, that has remained constant ever since. The trio then had a short break before working on *The Calling* (2003) which very quickly gained positive media attention including a five-star review in the *Daily Telegraph* (Frilingos 2003: S26), and a mention in the Global Pulse section of *Billboard* magazine (Eliezer 2004: 59). Prior to and during this

---

[11] Debris was also a part of the Adelaide group Cross Bred Mongrels. Alongside his DJ and production role in the Hilltop Hoods he also raps on some tracks.

[12] Although the track 'Walk On' from *The Calling* features DJ Next.

period, the Hoods were managed by PJ Murton from Pulling Strings Productions[13] who worked with the group from 1995 to 2008. They are currently managed by Dylan Liddy from Blue Max Music.

The Hoods had been developing their sound, stage presence and underground networks for a long time before the breakthrough of *The Calling*. Pressure said in 2004 that people had been making Hip-Hop music in Australia for 'a good 10 years' and this meant there had been 'time to build strength and the quality of the product is there now' (McMenemy 2004a: 9). This solid foundation was certainly required in Adelaide, which was not a major media or music centre in Australia, meaning that Hip-Hop artists had to build a scene without 'mainstream support' (Suffa in Hegarty 2003: 17). As I will discuss throughout this book, this underground community was suspicious of those they perceived as outsiders like major record labels, meaning that people valued being independent. This can be seen in

---

[13] Pulling Strings Productions (PSP) was a record label, distribution, management, event production and promotions business that was launched by PJ Murton. Kirk Wray and other unnamed collaborators joined the PSP team not long after, due to the need for expansion in live music events and distribution activities. Later on, the distribution arm was separated out, re-named 'Six Degrees Distribution' and run by Kirk Wray, who was also the manager of Adelaide group the Funkoars. As far as I am aware, this re-organization was amicable. PJ Murton still uses the Pulling Strings name to continue conducting music business, specializing in music industry consultation and advice. The 'behind the scenes' work of both PJ and Kirk needs to be acknowledged in accounts of Hip-Hop in Adelaide.

footage from *The Calling Live* (2005) where the Hoods discuss their plan to 'keep their souls' by remaining 'loyal to Obese'.

The Hoods toured extensively to promote *The Calling* and their subsequent album *The Hard Road* was the first Australian Hip-Hop release to debut at number one on the ARIA charts. Maya Jupiter said in a 2006 interview that the success of *The Hard Road* was a 'massive deal for Aussie hip hop' and that it made people 'feel proud' because it 'means the entire scene has come a long way' (Vaughan 2006: 9). The Hoods' success also shifted opinions within the music industry. Major labels now saw investing in locally produced Hip-Hop as a more viable market strategy, beyond token attempts to try and 'look for Eminem Part 2' (DJ Peril in Pollard 2004b: 49). This new-found interest was not welcomed by all Hip-Hop fans and artists, and I explore this further in the chapters that follow.

As of 2022, the Hoods have released ten full-length albums, their most recent being *The Great Expanse* in 2019. This was their sixth album to reach number one on the ARIA charts, a record for an Australian group (Gougoulis 2019). At the time of writing, they have recently released two new singles and are conducting a national tour titled 'The Show Business Tour'. The name of the tour is a reference to the single, 'Show Business ft. Eamon'. This was their first single since the 2020 charity release 'I'm Good?' which raised funds to support members of the music industry who had been impacted by the COVID-19 pandemic. As the title, 'Show Business' suggests, the new release ruminates on how their lives, including relationships with the music industry and fans, have changed as they have become more famous. One significant shift has been their ability to purchase professional recording equipment and expand their home studios. The Hoods have always had a strong DIY ethos, with *The Calling* being recorded and mixed at DJ Debris' home studio. Pressure described this process, explaining that the album was:

> largely produced on Suffa's mum's computer, we recorded the vocals in Debris' mum's bathroom. We set a mic up in there and the tiles gave it a nice natural reverb, which of course being professional music makers now, we would never dream of recording in anything but a dead soundproof studio room. It's so funny to think that we actually managed to come up with on what we made back then with such a minimal set up and no budget.
>
> (Tokatly 2019)

Interestingly, the computer that they used only had one speaker, which meant that the album was mono (Double J 2017). Most tracks on *The Calling* are produced by Suffa under the name 'Suffering City Productions'. Three songs are produced by Debris and 'The Certificate' is produced by Dazastah from Perth Hip-Hop group Downsyde. When I re-listened to the album in preparation for writing this book, I found that it had a stripped-back, sparse sound which is highly nostalgic for me and has become a valued aesthetic in itself. In the chapters that follow, I explore the sound, structure and lyrics of individual tracks from the album in more detail. These chapters build on the account of the histories of Hip-Hop in Australia and the formation of the Hilltop Hoods that I have set out here, providing a picture of the 2000s scene.

3 Hip-Hop devotion: 'Testimonial Year' and 'The Calling'

The Calling title track just brings all the other tracks together. It's like the captain of a sports team in the centre of a team photo. All the players on the team are good but the captain is what brings it together. It just grabs everyone together and goes, 'Come on. Let's go.' I think it encapsulated the whole album.

(Beats)

Like all the Hoods' albums to date, the cover of *The Calling* features a character who is called 'Armageddon'. According to the Hilltop Hoods' website, the cover image depicts Armageddon 'scaling the mountains to answer the calling' (Hilltop Hoods Website, 'Armageddon' n.d.). In this chapter, I explore this iconography and the two opening tracks of the album. I show that Hip-Hop as a calling and a religious devotion are themes that run across the album but are best exemplified by the title track and 'Testimonial Year'.

Introducing themselves

'Testimonial Year' is a jazzy, piano-led number that is essentially a mini-history of the group that introduces their love for Hip-Hop culture. For example, the track discusses when DJ Next left the group and Debris joined, how travelling to perform across Australia has affected their romantic relationships, and the challenges of navigating the business aspects of music production. The song's overall message and tone is perhaps best summed up by the word 'testimonial'. It is an expression of gratitude to their families, partners, manager, fellow Hip-Hop producers, fans, record stores, and many others who have helped them across their careers. It is also evidence of their commitment to Hip-Hop. Like several tracks on *The Calling*, the song describes participation in Hip-Hop culture as a form of religious devotion. In 'Testimonial Year', this includes Pressure rapping about the need to maintain the 'purity' of Hip-Hop in Australia, an issue that I return to in Chapter 6.

All the verses open with the refrain 'let me introduce myself' and the call for audience members to 'raise them beers' as if they were toasting the group. As the song progresses, Pressure and Suffa introduce themselves through their rhymes while Debris does so through turntablism as he cuts, scratches and juggles. The lyrics of 'Testimonial Year' establish that this is not the Hoods' debut album. The content focuses on the time and energy that the group have put into honing their music, detailing their hardships and successes across a career that already spans over ten years. According to journalist Luke Girgis, the self-referential nature of the song made it the 'perfect introduction [*sic*] track for newcomers to the group and genre' (Girgis 2019). Girgis included 'Testimonial Year' in a list of his top ten Hoods tracks for Tone Deaf, an Australian music news outlet. He wrote that it 'really painted a picture of exactly what the Australian Hip Hop scene was like through the 90's and early 00's. Testimonial Year is the Genesis [*sic*] of Australian Hip Hop for many fans nationally' (Girgis 2019).

'Testimonial Year' was the first single released from *The Calling* and the only song which had an official film clip (Hilltop Hoods 2007) until 2022 when the group released one for 'The Nosebleed Section' (Hilltop Hoods 2022). This suggests that the group and their management were surprised by the success of 'Dumb Enough?' and 'The Nosebleed Section'. The 'Testimonial Year' film clip features the Hoods performing to a small but dense crowd on a stage in front of a red velvet curtain and chandeliers that are suspended from the ceiling. The rest of the clip is intercut with footage of Pressure and Suffa rapping in front of a white background and scenes where all group members are travelling in a limousine drinking champagne with women. Near the end of the clip, the limousine pulls up to the venue which has an illuminated light box on the façade with lettering that reads 'The Sentinel' on the top line and 'Hilltop Hoods' on the next. This is an easter egg reference to the song 'The Sentinel' discussed in the conclusion. An easter egg is a hidden image or reference in electronic media that only astute fans will notice. In this case, the easter egg does not reveal anything, it is just an insider nod to the knowledgeable viewer. The clip concludes with the Hoods being replaced by young look-a-likes who finish the gig and walk back out to the waiting limousine. This could be another reference to how long the group had been making Hip-Hop, but to me it also implies that the members of the group are now realizing their childhood dreams.

Although 'Testimonial Year' did not become the breakthrough single, the song played an important role on the album by laying out the Hoods' ideology and history. Keep in mind that this was a pre-streaming era when people frequently purchased albums and listened to them in the track order set out by the artist. In his interview, MITUS noted that music piracy was very prevalent at this time, but Hoods' fans were proud of purchasing the album to support the group instead of illegally downloading songs. This pride in local Hip-Hop reverberates through 'Testimonial Year'. It made the song both the perfect introductory track for new listeners and an affirmation for existing Hip-Hop fans and artists. It celebrated the experiences of Hip-Hop practitioners who had been working to build Hip-Hop collectives in Australia, whilst also making these stories and histories accessible to a new cohort. As Maya Jupiter explained it 'talks about the culture, the community and what it takes to realise one's dreams. It's hard work and the love of the culture'.

While the Hoods were not widely known outside of the Hip-Hop scene in 2003, 'Testimonial Year' was a nod to the 'underground heads' who, like the Hoods, had been making Hip-Hop in Australia for several years. This message resonated with other artists like Ben Iota who saw themselves as being 'one of those people who were supporting [Hip-Hop] before it blew up'. Similarly, Tomahawk from Clandestien said that 2003 felt like the culmination of everything that Hip-Hop artists had been striving for. For him, it was a year of personal achievement with the release of Clandestien's album *Dynasty* (2003), and for the scene as a whole: 'it's what we were building towards. Every show, every album was a step towards something great and 2003 it exploded. The years leading up to that year were truly special – we all felt it. We were hungry and creative. We were full of hope and promise.' This creativity, hope and hunger are captured on the jubilant 'Testimonial Year' and are further developed on the title track of the album, 'The Calling', which sets out how the Hoods see themselves and their relationship to Hip-Hop culture.

Answering the call

> It's our calling that's why we say
> You got to pray, to Hip-Hop almighty
> (Chorus – 'The Calling')

As seen in the above excerpt from the chorus, the title track from the album describes Hip-Hop as a God-like, 'almighty' religious entity that the Hoods are worshipping through prayer and song. The track cleverly incorporates religious terms and imagery to convey the central role that Hip-Hop plays in their lives and their dedication to it. In particular, Pressure's first verse and the chorus of the song include a number of phrases associated with Roman Catholicism – stigmata, sacrifice, bless, Holy Father – that all work together to demonstrate how seriously the Hoods take Hip-Hop. The track suggests that group members have been 'called' to be Hip-Hop artists in the same way that other people are called by God/s or their faith to take on a religious vocation. Several academic studies have explored how diverse religions like Islam, Christianity and Rastafarianism have influenced Hip-Hop artists (c.f. Zanfagna 2015) but there is less work that considers how and why Hip-Hop artists draw on religion as an analogy for Hip-Hop. I want to stress here that I am not suggesting that the members of the Hilltop Hoods necessarily practise Catholicism or Christianity. Rather, I am highlighting that they are comparing the experience of Hip-Hop to the experience of religion. This tells us something interesting about how they understand Hip-Hop culture and their embodied, ritualistic relationship to it.

Because I did not interview the Hilltop Hoods, I cannot say conclusively what they were trying to convey through this song. However, it is not a stretch to say that the central message of the song is the all-consuming nature of their relationship with Hip-Hop culture – it informs every aspect of their lives.[1] It is an addiction that they cannot stop thinking about and a habit that they cannot give up. 'The Calling' viscerally describes how Hip-Hop engages their senses and affects their bodies. I was able to observe and experience these bodily responses and emotions first-hand when I was doing ethnographic research in Adelaide and Melbourne from 2006 to 2008 which included twenty-seven interviews with Hip-Hop artists/fans and attending numerous Hip-Hop gigs. During this research, people consistently and passionately told me how much they loved Hip-Hop. Like the lyrics of 'The Calling', two people that I interviewed, a 28-year-old MC and a 30-year-old Hip-Hop manager, directly compared Hip-Hop to religion. In a more contemporary example, when I interviewed MITUS for this project he said that while he was 'not a religious person', Hip-Hop was 'the closest thing to religion for me'. These comparisons were ways of articulating the reverence they had for Hip-Hop culture.

In my experience, this reverence can also result in people wanting to protect and control how Hip-Hop is represented and to prove their 'insider' status. For example, some of the lyrics in 'Testimonial Year' and 'The Calling' talk about the truthfulness and realness of the Hoods who are contrasted with other crews who are fake. It is now a well-worn cliché to say that debates about 'realness' and 'authenticity' often

---

[1] I would also add, that apart from guest features, all the lyrics across the album are written by either Pressure or Suffa and here I am conflating their individual points of view. While Debris is also an MC, I do not know if he has any input into Suffa's or Pressure's lyrics.

dominate discussions of Hip-Hop culture. However, any cursory look at the lyrics found on *The Calling* demonstrates why. The binary of real versus fake is constructed in multiple, overlapping ways across the album. People who are 'fake' are unskilled, lack commitment, do not fully understand or respect Hip-Hop and try to profit from Hip-Hop culture without giving back. Specifically, in these two tracks, the Hoods stress that they perform Hip-Hop because they love the craft and not because they want to achieve financial gain.

While claims made by musicians about their 'realness' and rejections of 'commercialization' are often rightly received with scepticism, when *The Calling* was released being able to make a full-time living as a Hip-Hop practitioner in Australia was a pipe dream. It was akin to the US era of Hip-Hop when artists like Grand Master Flash simply could not fathom that there would be an audience for 'a record re-recorded onto another record with talking on it' (George 2004: 52). Pre-*The Calling*, Pressure was writing lyrics for the album while being a new father trying to stay awake at a night-job (Tran 2021) and Suffa and Debris were also juggling work commitments. In this context, it is not surprising that they released a song that detailed the sacrifices they were making to create music. These religious themes of sacrifice and devotion were not isolated to lyrics alone. They were also replicated in the artwork for the album.

Armageddon: Hip-Hop warrior

In the introduction to the chapter, I described the illustrated character 'Armageddon' who is the core visual motif linking all the Hilltop Hoods' releases. This character was created by illustrator John Engelhardt who is a high school friend of Suffa and Pressure. Information about Armageddon is included on the Hilltop Hoods' website and in a featurette on the *City of Light* (2007). In the featurette, Engelhardt explains that the character is the 'visual representation of what the Hoods are about'. He also says that the initial idea for the character came from Suffa who gave him a brief describing the character as an 'urban warrior with two swords' (*City of Light* 2007). Armageddon is a mascot like Iron Maiden's 'Eddie' who was an influence on Suffa: 'I was an Iron Maiden fan, and they've got Eddie, who's a character that is on their tour posters, albums […] we were inspired by it' (Taylor 2019).

Armageddon first appeared on the release *A Matter of Time*, and this informed his name which comes from the 'cataclysmic nature of the lyrical content on the title track' (Hilltop Hoods Website, 'Armageddon' n.d.). The term 'Armageddon' has significance in both Christian and Islamic theologies, denoting the symbolic or literal place of a final battle between good and evil that will result in the end of the world. In the Hoods' work, the character's appearance and surrounding environment are tailored to each album so that Armageddon 'embodies the theme and the subject' (Hilltop Hoods Website, 'Armageddon' n.d.). In the artwork for *The Calling* he is depicted as a warrior-like, almost-religious figure who is literally worshipping at the temple of Hip-Hop. On the album cover, he is back-lit standing in silhouette in a doorway as light streams through. He is holding a raised samurai-like sword and another sword is sheathed on his back.

In the CD booklet, there are several images of Armageddon including close ups of his face and eyes, him kneeling at the bottom of a large cliff face, climbing over rocks towards a temple in the distance and pushing open the temple door. He is also shown inside the temple, posing like a knight on bended knee with one sword. He is in front of a large pedestal decorated with engravings. At the top are a DJ figure and two turntables. The DJ has one hand on a spinning record and the other on the mixer. These images are also included on the back of the 2003 vinyl release. Together they tell the story of an urban warrior who is on a Hip-Hop journey. Given the themes of the title track it would be fair to call this journey a religious pilgrimage. After completing his arduous trek up a mountain, he pays his respects to Hip-Hop itself, represented by the DJ figure. These images work with the album content to suggest that Hip-Hop culture should be respected and treated with awe.

Yet, as I will unpack in later chapters, for some Hip-Hop practitioners this reverence can become problematic. It can result in fans and artists being dogmatic about how Hip-Hop culture *must be* practised and defined. In terms of this album, the Hoods themselves do not always take things so seriously. While 'Testimonial Year' and 'The Calling' are ideological and introspective songs, the third track on the album is the comedic and boastful 'Dumb Enough?'. As I discuss in the next chapter, this song and 'The Nosebleed Section' were anthems that caught the attention of people outside of the Hip-Hop scene, helping to propel the Hoods into the national spotlight.

4 Punchlines and funky beats – 'Dumb Enough?' and 'The Nosebleed Section'

I really love Dumb Enough? Love it. […] just that beat, the production on it and the Hoods always deliver lyrically […] That's probably my favourite on there.

(Dazastah)

If you type 'swan' and 'Hilltop Hoods' into an internet search engine you will see a range of unlicensed merchandise featuring origami paper swans. These seemingly random items are references to a now-infamous line from the track 'Dumb Enough?' where Suffa says that he can make origami out of other MCs' lyrics. Pressure then asks Suffa what he has created, and he exclaims 'It's a swan!'. This line has taken on a life of its own and has been popular since the album's release. For example, Beats said that when he thinks back on *The Calling* launch, a memory that sticks in his head is 'just hearing 800 people[1] go "it's a swan!" […] I went, fuck man they have made it'. To this day, people still bring inflatable swan pool toys to Hoods festival gigs and reference it in memes. People also yell the line at Suffa when they see him. This has become so

---

[1]   As I discuss in Chapter 5, the capacity of the album launch venue was 2,000 plus people.

common that in 2019 during a live performance of 'Leave Me Lonely' for triple j's *Like A Version* series (triple j 2019) he said: 'if you see me in the street with my daughter, please don't yell out of your car window, "It's a swan"'. After the video was released, the Hilltop Hoods' twitter account, presumably run by Suffa, tweeted that he was worried he had only made the situation worse (@Hilltophoods Twitter 2019).

The fervour that some people have for this line is no doubt frustrating for Suffa and it is unfortunate that he needed to protect his daughter from being frightened by enthusiastic fans. From a purely analytical point of view, the impetus to yell this line is representative of both Pressure and Suffa's ability to craft memorable, shoutable punchlines that engage their audience. In this chapter, I explore this phenomenon, delving into the punchlines, catchy choruses and funky beats that make 'Dumb Enough' and 'The Nosebleed Section' fan favourite tracks. I analyse the lyrical themes and structure of these songs and provide some information about how they were produced. These songs highlight the key role that rhyme writing, production and live performance skills have played in the Hoods' career.

'It's a Swan!': Punchlines and lyrical structure

In relation to Hip-Hop lyrics, the word 'punchline' means a 'strong phrase in the lyrics that "punches", or hits, the listener. It can be something funny, an interesting metaphor or simile, clever wordplay, or anything that makes an impact' (Edwards 2009: 58). It is also aptly described as a term borrowed from comedy that refers to a line where 'all the elements of the previous lines come together' (Cobb 2007: 88). This highlights why the release experienced in a punchline can be so satisfying. It resolves a premise that has been set up in earlier lines. The swan line is one example of many punchlines across *The Calling*. Punchlines are essential in MC battles, where the goal is to mock and humiliate your opponent with your wordplay (Kautny 2015: 102). The lyrics of 'Dumb Enough?' fit neatly into this genre – the song could be classified as a battle-rap or a braggadocio Hip-Hop track. Its premise is critiquing other groups who are 'dumb enough' to try and challenge the Hilltop Hoods. It is a rhetorical question – are you dumb enough?

The track is also a good example of the rhyme patterns and song structures that the Hoods use across the album. It features verses that alternate between Pressure and Suffa, with the other MC who is not taking the lead often 'punching' or reinforcing the punchline by rapping it as well. Sometimes DJ Debris also plays this role. Unlike some other songs on the album, in 'Dumb Enough?' Pressure and Suffa also alternate lines within verses for emphasis. In terms of rhyme scheme itself, on *The Calling* the two MCs often use traditional rhyming couplets with the rhyme placed at the end of two paired lines. They also use a mix of perfect and imperfect or 'slant' rhymes. That is, sounds that do not rhyme perfectly but are similar.[2] For example, in 'Dumb Enough?', swan is rhymed with 'bomb'. Their rhymes tend to be mono-syllabic but they do use some multi-syllabic rhymes. They also use other techniques like internal rhymes and alliteration.

For some Hip-Hop practitioners, the use of densely layered, multi-syllabic rhymes is indicative of an MC's skill. The genesis

---

[2]   A poetic equivalent is assonance.

of multi-syllabic rhyming is typically traced back to US MC Rakim, who is a member of the acclaimed group Eric B and Rakim and a successful solo artist (Price-Styles 2015: 15). MCs like Rakim popularized rhyme structures and schemes that led to a new era of rhyming innovation. Although lyrical complexity has now become a marker of perceived quality and skill, there are numerous other factors that Hip-Hop aficionados consider when they rate MCs, including subject matter, story-telling ability, rhythm and speed. I believe that part of the Hoods' success can be attributed to the clarity of their rhymes. They enunciate words very clearly which enables people to follow along and they each have their own tone and flow. Several people I spoke to said that they enjoyed the complementary nature of Suffa and Pressure's distinctive flows and the smoothness of their rhymes.

As seen in the swan example, the Hoods also work numerous jokes, double entendre, similes and metaphors into their lyrics. These punches are particularly important in live shows, where they become moments for crowd participation. Live performance is a central aspect of MCing. Indeed, the word is an abbreviation of the term 'Master of Ceremonies', meaning someone that hosts events. I have attended several Hilltop Hoods shows, the first one being their 2005 show at the Adelaide University Cloisters. The most recent was the 'Speaking in Tongues National Tour' in 2012, which I attended in both Adelaide and my hometown Mildura.[3] At these gigs I have seen first-hand the sheer joy that people feel when they yell a line in unison with other audience members and the

---

[3] After this, my partner and I had children and my involvement with the Hip-Hop scene in Adelaide slowed down considerably.

Hilltop Hoods themselves.[4] This can clearly be seen in footage from *The Calling Live* (2005) where people are audibly rapping along with many lyrics. As I will show in Chapter 6, the Hoods' ability to 'rock a party' (Hegarty 2003: 17) was a key tool in their arsenal that contributed to the success of festival favourites like 'Dumb Enough?' and 'The Nosebleed Section'. As mentioned in the Introduction of the book, both of these tracks charted in the triple j 'Hottest 100' and the station named *The Calling* 'Album of the Week'. DJ Debris thought that without triple j support the Hoods 'would have sold half as many units' (Yeaman and McMenemy 2005: 46). In the final part of this chapter, I look at the popularity of the 'The Nosebleed Section' in more detail and trace some of its musical similarities with 'Dumb Enough?'.

Funky samples: Open doors

> The Nosebleed Section changed the landscape of hip hop in this country and heavily influenced many projects after this.
>
> (Shaker 2016)

The accolades of 'The Nosebleed Section' are too many to list in this book. It is recognized as a significant Australian song by national cultural institutions, journalists and Hip-Hop practitioners themselves. For example, it is part of

---

[4] This kind of communal participation is not unique to Hip-Hop, see for example Stratton's (2023) discussion of crowd members singing along in unison during Hunters and Collectors performances.

the curated collection 'A Taste of Sounds of Australia' by the National Film and Sound Archive of Australia (n.d.) alongside songs by legends like Archie Roach, AC/DC and John Williamson. It is frequently included in lists of the 'best' Australian Hip-Hop tracks or histories of Hip-Hop music from Australia (see Lal 2019). Reflecting its ongoing resonance with a triple j audience, in 2013 it was voted fourth in the 'Hottest 100 of the Past 20 Years' (triple j n.d.). In 2020, it topped Tone Deaf's list of fifty greatest Australian Hip-Hop songs of all time and was described as 'one of the most defining songs of an entire genre' (Jenke 2020/2021). The satirical Australian news website the Betoota Advocate even published a piece stating that Australians had decided that it should replace 'Advance Australia Fair' as the national anthem (Overell n.d.).

In 2005, Suffa noted that 'The Nosebleed Section' had 'done good things for us, opened doors for us' (*The Calling Live* 2005). Yet, this track almost did not make the album. It was recorded later than many other tracks and Suffa thought that it did not fit the overall vibe of *The Calling*: 'I really don't know what it is about that track – I can't put my finger on it. I was going to leave it off the album. I wanted to drop it off but Debris and Pressure wouldn't let me' (Young 2004: 35). The fact that the song made the album almost seems fated, particularly when you hear Suffa explain that he nearly left the record that he sampled to create it at a restaurant. Luckily, 'the restaurant owner chased me down the road and gave it back to me, so if he hadn't chased me down the road, I would have never made that song' (Double J 2017).

The record that he is talking about is Melanie Safka's 1972 album *Garden in the City,* released under the mononym 'Melanie'. On triple j (Tran 2021), Suffa explained that he bought the record for fifty cents ($AUD) in a thrift shop.[5] On first listen, he fell in love with the track 'People in the Front Row' which would become the musical backbone of 'The Nosebleed Section'. In the chorus of Safka's song, she sings about looking into the audience and falling in love with the 'people in the front row'. Suffa uses this sampled lyric to give props to the people who fill up the front row at Hip-Hop events, which he calls the nosebleed section. He has been criticized for failing to understand the meaning of the phrase 'nosebleed section' or 'nosebleeds', typically used to describe seats at an event that are far away from the front of the stage. That is, seats so high up in the back rows of a stadium that you might get a nosebleed from the shift in altitude. However, he has stressed that he chose the term deliberately to subvert its original meaning. At a Hip-Hop show, the 'nosebleeds' are not the back rows but the front rows where everyone is enjoying the show and getting rowdy (Tran 2021).

Initially, Suffa was perplexed that Safka's song had not already been used by another artist but he soon realized it was challenging to adapt:

> My first thought was like 'Why hasn't anyone used this before?' […] And when I started chopping the bass line, I realised why, the timing on it was real wild and it was hard to make it work […] With the drums as far as I remember, I found a break and I threw that on and I popped some kicks and snares over the top of that just to strengthen it and I cut it up to change the rhythm of it to suit the bass line.
>
> (Tran 2021)

---

[5] Thrift shops are also referred to as second-hand stores in Australia.

This short description of production techniques gives some useful insight into the Hoods' music-making process. As DJ Debris explained in 2003: 'we're more sample based [*sic*] than some crews […] A lot of our stuff tends toward the main vibe from an old funk track. But we do add in a lot of our own riffs, bass lines, keyboards, and we have session musos like horn players. We've had a bloke come in with an old Rhodes organ' (Dullroy 2003: 50).

Both 'Dumb Enough?' and 'The Nosebleed Section' are based around funky samples that are re-worked. These tracks are also more light-hearted and playful than other songs on the album. This playfulness was highlighted by DJ Debris who described 'Dumb Enough?' as being representative of their musical style at this time: 'It's got the vibe of the beat, the swing, a humorous "don't take life too seriously" kind of thing' (Dullroy 2003: 50). Similarly, Suffa explained that *The Calling* reflected a stylistic shift for the group: 'we used to do more melancholy tracks, with slower beats, but this album is a bit more of an up-tempo, battle-styled, party record. […] We take the piss out of ourselves on this album. It's probably more casual' (Colman 2003: 21). These changing influences mean that *The Calling* is a balanced mixture of socially conscious tracks, concept songs like 'The Calling' and 'The Sentinel', and, light-hearted party tracks.

Whatever the tone of the individual track, the Hoods have become well known for their compelling song structure which is clearly demonstrated on *The Calling*. As Ben Iota said: 'they were one of the first local groups I can remember thinking, these guys are making *songs* […] They've got choruses, everything has dynamism to it. It's structured and thought out and seems like everything that they were doing had a purpose. Every song was scrutinized and framed. You could tell it was a team effort.' Here Ben Iota highlights that the Hoods are skilled song writers as well as Hip-Hop lyricists. These skills are showcased on 'Dumb Enough?' and 'The Nosebleed Section', tracks which are humorous and funky. These attributes mean that they are memorable songs that are easy to sing and remain crowd favourites at performances. As I discuss in the next chapter, the Hoods are highly professional, engaging live performers and this has been a key factor in their success. As Suffa proclaimed: 'our shows convert people' (Eliezer 2004: 59).

5 Rocking the party: Live performances

The year is 2004 or possibly 2005[1], my memory is becoming hazy. What remains clear is the feeling of anticipation as I gather with a throng of eager fans to see the Hilltop Hoods perform at the Adelaide leg of the national Big Day Out (BDO) tour. As more and more fans arrive, people are pushing forward to see the stage and jostling for space. The crowd roars as the Hoods take the stage and begin performing. Pressure and Suffa race around the stage, commanding the crowd. Their energy is intense. The bass from the massive sound system booms in our chests. As the set unfolds, we watch on with a mix of horror and enthusiasm when a determined fan tries to get a better view by climbing onto the roof of a nearby pavilion. We cheer, gasp and laugh as this rebel is chased across the roof by a security guard in a very precarious situation. Welcome to a Hilltop Hoods show.

This chapter features accounts of Hilltop Hoods' performances from the early 2000s including key Adelaide events and their national tour. Across interviews for this book, the Hoods' dedication to rehearsing and honing their live shows was a recurring theme that was linked to their ongoing success.

---

[1] From my memory, this occurred at the 2004 BDO which also included Afrika Bambaataa on the line-up. However, unofficial sources that I consulted said that the Hoods did not perform in 2004. The BDO was a celebrated national Australian music festival that began in 1992 and ran until 2014.

While the national popularity of *The Calling* was instigated by radio play, it was consolidated by the Hoods' enigmatic live performances across Australia.

Launching *The Calling* (Planet nightclub)

The Hilltop Hoods released *The Calling* on 22 September 2003 and launched it at an event at the now-defunct Planet nightclub in Adelaide on 4 October. According to the description in the Adelaide newspaper *The Advertiser* (2003: 63), the line-up was massive, consisting of Adelaide music groups, DJs and Breakers alongside artists from Perth, Sydney and Melbourne: 'Pegz, Layla, DJ Bonez, Hyjak, Torcha, Funkoars, Train of Thought, Da Klinic Breakers and Certified Wise, DJs Reflux, Snair, Dyems, Kim Dezen, David L, Shep and Kirk, Hosted by Reason and Fatface'. This event was an 'all-ages' gig with a dedicated area for people who were under eighteen upstairs. I was able to interview six people who attended or performed at the Planet show. Beats, Ben Iota, Chris Bass, DJ Sanchez and Kultar Ahluwalia attended the event as Hip-Hop fans/artists and Layla performed on the line-up. Chris Bass explained that the launch was sold-out, and the venue may have been over its official capacity of 2,125 people.[2] Hopeful fans who did not have tickets were 'queued back for a block outside trying to get in' (Chris Bass).

For some of the younger Hip-Hop artists that I interviewed, this event was a source of inspiration and one of their first

---

[2] The information about the venue's capacity was sourced after the interview by Chris.

introductions to Hip-Hop created by Australians. Kultar was fifteen at the time and it was the first music show that he had attended without a family member. He said that a 'real clear highlight' of the event was 'seeing the Hoods do the posse cut from the album, 'The Certificate', with everyone on stage at once'. DJ Sanchez had just turned nineteen and it was the first local Hip-Hop show that he attended. It significantly changed his perception of Hip-Hop in Australia:

> It was just an epic event. […] after that I was just like […] Jesus Christ, these guys are professional rap musicians, but they're from Blackwood. And they're doing it like the pros […] that was a big eye-opening moment. I think not just for me, but for anybody. I've interviewed dudes on the channel [The Lesson 92.7] that were there, like other artists and they'll all say that was an eye-opening moment, where everyone was just like, this is real. This is really a *thing*. And then after that they [Hilltop Hoods] just took off and never slowed down.

One of the people that DJ Sanchez interviewed was MC Flak aka Fatface from the Cross Bred Mongrels who helped host the show with Melbourne MC Reason. Flak said that the event was packed and that people were even hanging from rafters: 'the vibe was crazy, it was a serious gig' (The Lesson W/ DJ Sanchez 2017a). Like DJ Sanchez, Flak indicated that the success of this event spurred the realization that it was possible to have a career as a Hip-Hop artist in Australia.

For Layla, the launch night coincided with her twenty-first birthday party and was an 'epic' night. At the time, it was the largest crowd she had performed for and she felt 'honoured'. She already knew the Hilltop Hoods from events in Perth, including a show at the Paddington Ale House that 'drew a big crowd for the time' with tickets only costing '$4.50 which included a beer, wine or champagne'. In contrast, *The Calling* album launch was a symbol of the growing popularity of the Hoods, which Layla summed up as 'forever increasing'.

Both Beats and Ben Iota (formerly Bornski) had been involved in the Adelaide scene before *The Calling*, first as Hip-Hop fans and then creating Hip-Hop themselves. In 2003, they were already making music with people who would go on to become the group Adroit Effusive (*Adroit Effusive: The Album* 2010), albeit with some line-up changes. They both saw this event as an important turning point for the Adelaide scene and Hip-Hop more broadly. Beats had been a fan of the Hoods since well before *The Calling*, having written a letter to their P.O. Box which he found on the back of *A Matter of Time* (1999). He loved the album – it was the catalyst that led to him becoming a Hip-Hop artist himself: 'that week, I went and got a computer, like I bought a computer and got a cracked version of Fruity Loops and just started'. Beats was not involved in the production of *The Calling* but he did help to promote it by working with other members of Adroit Effusive, Kirk Wray and PJ Murton to post event fliers on stobie poles, a South Australian term for electricity poles. The group 'met at the Blackwood post office. And back in the day, heaps of the boys worked for "Couriers Please" but Baz [DJ Debris …] had a van and they just had boxes and boxes and boxes of these posters'. After bombing the streets with posters, Beats described the Planet show as being 'huge': 'it was the biggest gig I'd seen at that time, ever' (Beats).

Like Beats, Ben Iota was listening to the Hoods when *A Matter of Time* (1999) was released. He described the album as being 'on par' with US Hip-Hop from Philadelphia, New York and Boston that he was listening to in the 1990s. By the time

The Calling was launched, Ben was performing at Hip-Hop events and participating in freestyle battles. He recalled that the Planet launch brought the Adelaide Hip-Hop community 'out of the woodwork': 'it was more people at a local gig than I'd ever seen, by far. Everyone who was in the scene before *Calling* dropped, was there. Like it brought everyone out.' While the positive reception at the Planet gig boded well for the Hoods, by the time they played the 2,000 capacity Thebarton Theatre in November 2004, the success of the album had well and truly been cemented.

Fireworks and frenzy: Thebarton Theatre and National Tour

The Thebarton Theatre performance saw the Hoods step up their production even further.[3] Raph AL described the show as being 'nuts' and praised the Hoods' performance skills, comparing them to Def Wish Cast: 'every time that the Hoods play it's great. Because the only act in my eyes that can match what the Def Wish Cast energy does, is what the Hoods do.' The Thebarton show was filmed for the DVD *The Calling Live* (2005) and was hosted by MC Flak in a flawless white tracksuit. It was apparently the first time that a Hip-Hop group from Australia had used pyrotechnics in their show. Indeed, some of the people that I spoke to identified the show in this way: 'the pyrotechnics one?'. In his Lesson interview (The Lesson W/ DJ Sanchez 2017a), Flak spoke

---

[3]   Six people that I interviewed for this book attended the event: Beats, Ben Iota, Chris Bass, DJ Sanchez, Kultar and Raph AL.

about the key role that the Hilltop Hoods' manager PJ Murton played in organizing and filming this event: 'yeah PJ went all out on that one. I think he hired the camera, the boom camera from the ABC footy[4] coverage.' Kultar also described this step-up in production as being 'the first time I'd seen things really elevate in terms of stagecraft [...] big screens on the stage, fireworks [...] this was unheard of in Australian Hip-Hop at the time'. From Kultar's perspective, even though the Planet show was big, the Thebarton Theatre show was 'substantially bigger again'.

By this time, the Hoods' audience had expanded, according to Beats: 'there was a lot of young kids there. There was a lot of surfies, there was a lot of non-traditional Hip-Hop kids there.' For Beats, this event was a pivotal moment on both a personal and a professional level. As he watched the show and 'blazed up' in the back rows of Thebarton Theatre he said that he felt quite humbled. He was really happy for the Hoods' success and he felt like he was a part of it – not the Hoods career specifically – but the broader Hip-Hop community that they all came from. He explained that the Hoods were 'kicking the door open for us, for a while they were holding the door open'. By this he meant that not only did the success of the Hoods open new avenues for other Hip-Hop artists but that the Hoods actively helped to promote other groups. Ben Iota had a similar feeling as he watched the performance unfold. He said that he felt like:

> This thing is really popping off now, this is just amazing. Big things could happen, even for me, big things could happen [...] what I'm witnessing now is the world coming around

---

[4]   Australian Broadcasting Corporation. Footy is short for football.

> to what I've known for years, that this thing is great. I was actually happy to see it going so big, because all of a sudden […] I felt validated.

This sense of validation is significant because prior to this people who liked Hip-Hop in Australia were often mocked. For Ben, it felt like a shift not only for the acceptability of Hip-Hop culture but a much broader 'decentering of the conservatism of Adelaide, of its rock and roll past'.

After their triumphant performance at Thebarton Theatre, in 2005 the Hilltop Hoods became one of only three Adelaide acts, SuperJesus and Mark of Cain being the others, to play every Big Day Out festival show in each capital city (McMenemy 2004b: 12). Being selected to play each capital city on the tour was significant because smaller local acts were placed on the bill in their home state but did not travel with the festival. In Adelaide, the Hoods were received by a frenzied crowd: 'squished shoulder to shoulder with complete strangers, it was hard to breathe, let alone see the stage. Still, MCs Suffa and Pressure and DJ Debris came out, and buoyed by the hometown crowd, played the show of their lives' (McMenemy 2005: 8). This was a fantastic hometown reception, and it was echoed across Australia. According to Pressure, the group 'packed every stage so far to the point where people were trying to cram in' and Suffa added 'we've had people climbing trees and posts, trying to see' (McMenemy 2005: 8).

Overall, the Hoods toured *The Calling* for over a year and a half, performing around seventy shows including international events in London and South Korea (Young 2006: 27). The Hoods' energetic live shows from this era are captured in a new film clip for 'The Nosebleed Section' that was released in May 2022. This is the first film clip for the song released by the Hoods (Hilltop Hoods 2022), replacing an unofficial YouTube clip which was uploaded by user 'Bam05' and used 'The Nosebleed Section' as a backing track to BMX tricks (Bam05 2016). This unofficial clip has become well known amongst Hoods' fans and to date it has over twenty-three million views. The new official version is comprised of live performance footage from the BDO and other events, a grainy time-capsule of past hyped up crowds.

While this chapter has focused on Adelaide events, people that I interviewed from across Australia also shared memories of Hoods' gigs in their towns. For example, Ben Funnell (April77 Creative) attended the Canberra launch for *The Calling*. He said it was the first time that he had seen the Hoods live and even now he describes it as being 'one of the dopest live shows I've ever seen'. He said that people were crowd surfing at the show and the 'energy was undeniable […] the Hoods had total control of the audience'. Their ability to control the audience meant that the Hoods were able to win over fans when they supported international artists, who they sometimes upstaged. While they were already well-rehearsed, there is no doubt that this touring experience helped them to extend and perfect their performance skills.

Across their career, the Hoods have been able to maintain this high level of stagecraft and their shows have become more extravagant as they have gained access to larger budgets. For example, DJ Josie Styles described how she had performed at large events like Falls Festival where the Hoods were on the main stage: 'I played the smallest stage to like 10,000 people with KillaQueenz,[5] and then we've gone out and seen them for New Years, and they're like still fucking so deadly […] their performances are bloody amazing'. If there are any downsides

---

[5] KillaQueenz were a Sydney Hip-Hop duo comprised of Kween G and Desiree.

to this reputation for high-energy live performance, it is the perception that the Hoods are a 'festival' act who only produce light-hearted larrikin or party tracks. In the next chapter, I use an analysis of 'Walk On' and 'Illusionary Lines' to show that this is a simplification that does not reflect the diverse range of socio-political issues discussed on *The Calling*. I also consider how the ethos of independence shaped the album, demonstrating that like many underground Hip-Hop artists in Australia and internationally, the Hoods were suspicious of the impacts of commercialization on Hip-Hop culture.

6 Underground politics – 'Walk On' and 'Illusionary Lines'

Hip-Hop in Australia is now mainstream, but at the time The Calling dropped it was still a relatively small and underground community. The Calling was the first Australian Hip-Hop album to breakthrough to a wider audience on a major scale.

(Ben Funnell, April77 Creative)

More than a festival or larrikin act

In an interview conducted for this book, Mark Pollard said that the Hoods have 'played at a lot of festivals' but that this did not mean it would be 'fair to call them a festival act'. Mark did not listen to *The Calling* a lot when it was released because it was a time of many important life events for him including getting married. However, he re-listened to the album and other Hoods' songs in preparation for the interview, noting that the Hoods were 'writing about some really interesting issues, you know, the song, 'City of Light' (*The Hard Road 2006*), and 'Walk On' […] they were talking about the environment, talking about politics, talking about Australia being beholden to Bush [former President George W. Bush] and things like this'. Similarly, Maya Jupiter said that she was attracted to the song

'Walk On' because it related to the music that she loved which she described as 'politically minded' and 'socially conscious':

> The song talks about issues of the time and brings to light things that we need to improve on as a society. I think that's so important. You know, you can have your fun club songs and songs to drink to, but at the end of the day, for me, it's important to have a message in the music. I believe that's our job as artists.

As highlighted by Mark Pollard and Maya Jupiter, the verses in 'Walk On' comment on a broad range of environmental, social and political issues. This includes the Australian federal government's relationship with the United States, the morality of US military interventions, climate crisis and the treatment of asylum seekers. Suffa and Pressure each have one extended verse on the track. At the end of his verse, Suffa raps:

> Wanna affect change in the subjects that we talk on
> Connect strangers, work together, and walk on

This call for collective political action is a dimension of the Hoods' music that is not typically discussed in media or other academic accounts. For example, in an article about the history of Australian Hip-Hop, Kish Lal (2019) groups the Hilltop Hoods with 360 and Bliss n Eso, describing them as 'larrikin rappers' who 'employed their melodic Aussie lilts to songs about music festivals and drinking in the sun, charming their way into the cultural consciousness'.

This description of the Hoods draws on understandings of larrikinism that emerged towards the end of the First World War (Bellanta 2012). In her pre-war history of larrikins, Melissa Bellanta (2012: 6) demonstrates that 'larrikin' was initially a self-descriptor used by young people living in poverty in urban

Melbourne in the 1860s. By the late 1800s and early 1900s it had become a derogatory label employed by the media in a moral panic about 'rough youth' in Melbourne and Sydney (2012: xiv). It was not until the 1910s that 'claiming to be a larrikin or possessing a "larrikin streak" became acceptable outside adolescent street circles' (2012: 182). Since the 1930s, the term has been romanticized and connected to qualities like an irreverent sense of humour, distaste for authority, drunkenness and rowdiness – all underpinned by a 'heart of gold' (2012: xxi; xvi). In the afterword to her book, Bellanta notes that the term is predominantly used by men in their fifties and older, leading her to wonder if 'the larrikin myth will remain relevant in the future' (2012: 188). It is interesting to see that the concept lives on, in this case, being applied to Hip-Hop groups.

While Lal's (2019) use of the term seems to be positive, Tony Mitchell has been more critical of the messages in the Hoods' music. In 2007, he wrote that there was little in their lyrics that 'goes beyond the self-reflective and the dance and club-oriented' (Mitchell 2007: 109). He quotes a line from *The Hard Road* track 'Obese Lowlifes' (2006) where Suffa raps about his hatred for John Howard and Tony Blair, then Prime Ministers of Australia and the UK, respectively. For Mitchell (2007: 110), this line 'could be seen as a measure of their lack of sophistication in relation to far more politically conscious crews' such as Curse Ov Dialect, TZU and the Herd. I agree that the Hilltop Hoods are not well known for writing tracks that encourage direct political activism. That said, to characterize them as 'larrikins' or 'club-orientated' overlooks the diverse range of topics that they do discuss in their rhymes. For example, on the same album as 'Obese Lowlifes', Pressure has a solo track called 'Stopping All Stations' that tells the story of an elderly pensioner being robbed and stabbed on a train. The narrative unfolds through the eyes of three different people – the man himself, a woman who comes to his aid and the perpetrator. This track is classic Hip-Hop as socio-political commentary. It uses a tragic, fictionalized event to reflect on everyday struggles that many people in Australia face like poverty and battles with substance abuse. While it is not a political song with a 'capital P', that is, a song about macro-politics or governance, it is a micro-political song that encourages people to think critically about the world that they live in.[1]

Pressure's solo track 'Illusionary Lines' on *The Calling* fits into the same category. He explains that he wrote much of the song while he was at work and 'bored out of my fucking head' (*The Calling Live* 2005). Reflecting this boredom, the first verse describes the monotony of working in an unfulfilling job where writing rhymes is a reprieve that helps pass the time. The track invites people to critically reflect on the habitual routines and social expectations that shape their everyday lives. The listener is challenged to stop walking down 'illusionary lines'. Namely, to stop being a follower who blindly accepts the status quo without critical thought.[2] The chorus which is scratched by DJ Debris repeats a call for people to 'wake up' and 'rise up'. While the first verse focuses on the drudgery of working in an unrewarding job in a capitalist system, subsequent verses expand this focus to include debates about the impacts of industrialization on creativity. This final section of the song reflects the ideological ethos of underground and independent Hip-Hop.

---

[1] For an extended discussion of the politics of popular culture and a definition of micro-politics, see Fiske (2010: 6–9).
[2] While I don't follow these leads, there are clear links here to the work of theorists from the Frankfurt School who explored the impacts of 'mass culture' including whether there was scope for 'resistance' through popular culture.

Underground scene: Building support structures

Fears about Hip-Hop culture being exploited by undeserving artists or profiteering corporations were intense at the time that I conducted research for my PhD (2006–8) and were already burgeoning pre-*The Calling* as shown in lyrics across the album. This is reflective of the era, when there was a strong sense of community and camaraderie amongst Hip-Hop practitioners in Australia, particularly at the state and local level. For example, in Adelaide there was a high concentration of groups from the Southern suburbs who collaborated, as seen in the collective Certified Wise. At this time, people who were in business roles like media producers, record labels, distributors and owners of Hip-Hop stores were often Hip-Hop creators themselves. Of course, this is not to suggest that there were no interpersonal conflicts but rather to highlight the interconnected and dense nature of the relationships between Hip-Hop fans, artists, promoters and journalists in the late 1990s and early 2000s.

This was an era when Hip-Hop fans and artists were marginalized and were often stereotyped, mocked, and even physically attacked for their involvement in Hip-Hop culture. For example, at a recent panel for the Adelaide Hip-Hop festival Point of Contact,[3] former manager of the Hilltop Hoods PJ Murton said that when he was growing up you could get 'bashed' for being into Hip-Hop. Similarly, Chris Bass explained that in Blackwood there was a crew of 'older kids' who were called 'the ARC, the Anti-Rap Campaign'. The ARC hung out near the train station and

---

[3] This festival was organized by Thelements crew and ran from 22 to 31 July 2022 (see Point of Contact Festival 2022).

if you walked past them 'wearing baggy jeans or a baseball cap, you'd get bashed'. Over the years that I have been conducting research into Hip-Hop in Australia, numerous people have told me that when they started to get into Hip-Hop, they were one of a small handful of people in their school or social circle who were interested in it. As MC Raph AL explained, 'when I was coming up doing Hip-Hop, it wasn't cool to be a rapper'.

Given this context, it is unsurprising that many Hip-Hop practitioners identified as 'outsiders' and defined Hip-Hop as an oppositional counterculture or subculture. This was due to both the small-scale nature of the scene and the active dismissal of Hip-Hop by their peers and mainstream media outlets. As Maya Jupiter said, 'I'm from the era of, "we don't play rap crap on this [radio] station" [...] just being the butt of jokes and not even being respected as an Australian MC [...] And so those avenues were not open to us, you know? We had to fight for that shit'. Maya passionately described feeling like she had found her community when she attended a ten-day Sydney Hip-Hop festival called Urban Xpressions run by Trent Roden from Slingshot Entertainment, MC Trey, and Baba Israel of Metabass'n'Breath in 1998. At this same festival MC Quro – aka Andrew Bradley from Adelaide group Finger Lickin' Good[4] with MC Madcap and Producer/DJ Groove Terminator[5] – described

---

[4] Finger Lickin' Good were the first Adelaide Hip-Hop group to release vinyl, the EP *Illegitimate Sons of the Bastard Funk* (1993) (Downing 2006: 11). Madcap and Quro also ran important Hip-Hop events in Adelaide and with DJ Next and Sista Jane they launched the Hip-Hop radio show 93.7 Degreez in the Shade on 3D radio in 1995 (Downing 2006: 11).

[5] Groove Terminator was also in Major Rhyme Squad with MC Say. They were one of Adelaide's earliest Hip-Hop groups with others being Point Blank and Unit-E (Chris Bass).

Hip-Hop in Australia in the following way: 'We do not have any internal structures in this country. We do not have a record company that is devoted to pushing and promoting Australian talent, we do not have a national radio show, we do not have a national magazine. We do not, for the most part, have a great deal of contact between the cities' (Bradley 1999: 22).

Rather prophetically, MC Quro noted that if Hip-Hop practitioners were able to channel their energy, talent and support each other, there would come a time when 'there is a company who can distribute our material, when there is a magazine where you can read about our latest releases, where there is a TV show, where there is a radio show' (Bradley 1999: 22). Quro noted in his speech that people like himself and Madcap were putting in the work to support Hip-Hop practitioners and create this infrastructure. The dedication of figures like Madcap, Quro and many others meant that by 2003 when *The Calling* was released, several of these pieces had fallen into place.[6] I have already noted the impact of the launch of the national triple j Hip-Hop show in 2001 but here I also want to recognize other important factors that helped to promote Hip-Hop in Australia as set out by Arthur (2010: 93–5) in his ethnographic study of Adelaide Hip-Hop from 2002 to 2005.

In 2001, *Out4Fame* and *Stealth* magazine became 'fully fledged', full colour magazines with national distribution. In 2002, Mass MC created the website ozhiphop.com which

---

[6]   This labour was recognized by Ben Iota who spoke about Madcap's influence in Adelaide: 'He was bringing DJs over, he was putting on gigs, he was running battles, doing his radio show. He's working at Central Station [record store]'. This mention of Madcap and Quro is not meant to disrespect the contributions of many other people at this time.

included a forum. Prior to this, people were already using the internet to network in particular Internet Relay Chat (IRC) channels and state-based forums, but ozhiphop.com/forum became a central digital meeting place. Arthur (2010) also notes the significance of the release of the *Culture of Kings* compilations which I briefly introduced in Chapter 1. The influence of these compilations and their launch parties was reiterated by several people who I interviewed for this book. These events helped to connect people, who began to see themselves as part of a national Hip-Hop community: 'when *Culture of Kings* happened [...] because it was two things. It was kind of the compilation but then it was also the fact that then they put the big, national, kind of shows on in Adelaide first and then in Melbourne. That was monumental' (Dazastah). The 'monumental' impact of *Culture of Kings* was also stressed by Beats who said that it brought everyone together: 'that night I met Downsyde, Koolism, Mortar, Clandestien [...] that just blew it open, so that was a big thing for me' (Beats).[7]

As these quotes demonstrate, pre-*The Calling* in the late 1990s and early 2000s there was a strong sense of collective identity and shared experience amongst Hip-Hop fans and artists. This sense of cohesion extended beyond the national level, with Hip-Hop practitioners in Australia seeing themselves as being closely connected to underground or independent Hip-Hop in both the United States and other global Hip-Hop scenes like the UK. As Hip-Hop artists and fans in Australia were struggling to be respected, Hip-Hop in the United States was becoming increasingly corporatized.

---

[7]   Beats thought DJ Dyems did not get enough respect for his role in creating the *Culture of Kings* compilations: 'people don't even know it was him [...] he released that so selflessly'.

Illusionary lines: Independence and anti-commercialism

In his exploration of underground Hip-Hop in the United States, Christopher Vito (2019: 131–2) states that there was a period in the 1990s when major corporations started producing more Hip-Hop music and other products. In turn, this resulted in a wave of resistance from independent artists: 'the emergence of mainstream and company-controlled music has created a revival of an underground hip-hop culture. The use of independent media, such as small radio stations, the internet, small show venues and independent record stores, help to spread independent artists' music without filtering (or the selection process by corporate executives)' (Vito 2015: 318). The influence of underground Hip-Hop from the United States and United Kingdom meant that Australian artists and fans frequently denounced the materialism displayed in much 'mainstream' or corporatized Hip-Hop. This was despite there being very limited scope to make money from Hip-Hop in Australia at this point in time. I discussed this phenomenon with Ben Iota in our interview, saying that I thought some of these anti-commercialism themes were imported from US Hip-Hop. He agreed, indicating that it was what 'the underground fan base were accustomed to listening to, from underground American Hip-Hop, so the themes worked their way into local Hip Hop'.

In the 1990s and early 2000s, many Australians directly contrasted Hip-Hop in Australia with the commodification of much US Hip-Hop. For example, while Maya Jupiter said that while she would not use the term 'underground' today, in the past it was a phrase that she and other Hip-Hop practitioners used to differentiate themselves from 'people who loved commercial rap'. While Maya was cautious about not speaking for other members of the scene, she thought that Hip-Hop artists during this era did not really 'aspire to' the imagery used in mainstream 'million-dollar' US film clips, which often featured rappers wearing gold chains and driving luxury cars.[8] Because Hip-Hop practitioners in Australia were influenced by underground Hip-Hop, a strong emphasis was placed on being independent. In 2006, Pressure even compared Australian Hip-Hop to the US scene prior to significant involvement from major record labels:

> Australian hip hop is now at the stage that American hip hop was at about 10 or 15 years ago, which they classify as the golden era [...] So much raw but good-quality music is coming out of the scene. So far it's untainted by major labels. Everyone's really doing their own thing [...] International artists see our scene as very healthy and growing rapidly.
>
> (Wehner 2006: L14)

Here, major record labels are viewed with suspicion. Their involvement is seen as a potentially corruptive force that might 'taint' the scene.

These concerns are echoed in the lyrics of 'Illusionary Lines'. In the final verses, Pressure challenges people to think about the products that they are being sold by corporations and the mainstream media. He criticizes fashion and music industries for marketing commodities and lifestyles to people that are merely illusions which do not lead to personal fulfilment. He also voices concerns about Hip-Hop

---

8   In the year that *The Calling* (2003) was released the highest performing single in the United States was 50 Cent's 'In Da Club' (Billboard Top 100).

culture being marketed as a commodity by 'outsiders' who are not connected to it. As introduced in Chapter 3, this is a theme that is developed across the entire album. Artists who are committed to and love Hip-Hop like the Hilltop Hoods are frequently contrasted with others who have not paid their dues. In 'Illusionary Lines', Pressure explicitly denounces Hip-Hop crews who achieve fame and fortune without paying their debt to Hip-Hop:

> I once had respect for this game but now this game of respect
> Is sold to the highest bidder with some fame and a cheque

Such concerns about the commercialization of Hip-Hop can be linked back to the histories of the US Hip-Hop scene and the experiences of artists who felt exploited by restrictive contract offers. Independence was highly valued because it was equated with being able to retain control of your music and self-presentation. Indeed, when the Hilltop Hoods eventually left Obese Records and created their own record label, Pressure cited wanting to be able to manage the business aspect of their careers as the reason: 'we've always had control, but this just gives us the control over our music on a business level' (Coby 2009).

In addition to retaining control, independence was also closely connected to community values. It was linked to wanting to give back to Hip-Hop, to create for the culture and not for economic gain. I hope it has already become apparent that there were very strong ties between many Hip-Hop artists when *The Calling* was released. The friendships that were formed through Hip-Hop during this period were extremely meaningful and important to the people that I interviewed for this book. Other Hip-Hop artists were referred to as being 'family' and people got quite emotional when reflecting on the past, including remembering people who had died. As Suffa put it on the title track 'The Calling', Hip-Hop had given him a bed in every state of Australia. No matter where he travelled, he would have a place to stay because of his relationships with other Hip-Hop artists. This line was mentioned in several interviews that I conducted – it clearly resonated with people's own experience. For example, DJ Josie Styles explained that when she began booking more support act slots around Australia, she would call Hip-Hop artists from other states who were friends-of-friends to see if she could stay with them. They would always agree: 'mi casa su casa' – my house is your house.

As seen here, the close-knit nature of the Hip-Hop scene at this time had many positive implications. However, the flip side of this was a protectiveness that was not always productive. Having to fight to gain respect meant that Hip-Hop practitioners became very invested in how Hip-Hop was defined in Australia, who could produce it, and especially, who could profit from it. As Newcastle MC MITUS said: 'when Hip-Hop was having its moment [after the success of *The Calling*], we were quite defensive of it and for good reason, because, essentially we feel like we've fought for this'. This defensiveness enabled people to make distinctions between 'us' and 'them', drawing boundary lines around who was part of the community and who was not. Yet, for a period it also meant that people who experimented with Hip-Hop or did not follow 'the rules' were dismissed as being 'inauthentic'. This kind of policing of the scene was not supported by Mark Pollard who said:

> The positive side of the scene is, I don't know what it's like now. But a little bit like [...] if you played soccer or you did Brazilian Jiu Jitsu, you can travel around the world, and you'll

find a crew of people you can hang out with, and you're into the same thing. So that's cool. The scene when it comes to like, policing of the scene? Not cool.

This sentiment was shared by Maya Jupiter who laughed when I asked her about conservatism in the scene: 'it's so funny because, man, ohhhh, there were so many rules! It was like there was this invisible, Hip-Hop board. And they were deciding what Hip-Hop was. And I remember somebody saying, "If you sing in the chorus, it's not Hip-Hop"'.

As I discuss further in the conclusion of this book, as the Hoods became more commercially successful, they found themselves at the centre of debates about whether or not they had 'sold out' and were no longer following the 'Hip-Hop rules'. Before I look at these issues, I consider how *The Calling* was shaped by conventions that are common in battle rap, such as word play, metaphors and dissing opponents.

7 Posse tracks and battle raps – 'The Certificate'

I am a true believer that the essence of Hip-Hop is based on a person bettering themselves in every aspect of their lives. Battle style raps push the artist to cleverly craft witty and intelligent punchlines to demoralise their opponents. Achieving this in a braggadocio way only adds to their credibility and stature. It is directly comparable to a Graffiti artist styling their letters to have that funk and swing to them – leaving competitors jealous of what they can achieve style wise.

(Anthony Lewps)

As seen in the above quote from Lewps, battling to win respect and prove yourself is a core part of Hip-Hop culture. This battle ethos is highlighted on the posse track, 'The Certificate' that includes nineteen MCs and DJs from the Certified Wise crew all vying to outperform each other. In this chapter, I detail how this track was recorded and highlight the centrality of battling for status in the mid-2000s Hip-Hop scene.

Introducing posse tracks

There is a long and rich history of posse tracks in Hip-Hop, dating back to the 1980s. One classic that features on many 'best of' lists is 'The Symphony' (1988) by Queensbridge MC and producer Marley Marl. The track features verses by Big Daddy Kane, Kool G Rap, Craig G and Masta Ace. There is some debate amongst fans and artists about what constitutes a posse track. I have seen some lists that exclude Wu-Tang Clan tracks from 'posse track' status because all the artists are seen as being from the same group or collective. Technically this could also apply to Certified Wise tracks, but I do not think this distinction is helpful. I define a posse track as a song that features four or more verses or DJ cuts from different artists who are either part of a broader collective or who are solo artists/group members that do not typically perform together. Posse cuts usually have individual verses of around eight bars and minimal or no chorus.

I did not attempt to trace the first Australian posse track, but a contender might be the Def Wish Cast song 'Saga (Iron Fist)' which features Madcap, Merma, Mistery, Quro, Reason and Wizdm. This song, from the 1993 album *Knights of the Underground Table,* is seven minutes of intense rhymes. Raph AL mentioned this track as an early inspiration and Def Wish Cast and Adelaide crew Finger Lickin' Good as important figures in the history of Hip-Hop from his perspective: 'it's definitely Def Wish Cast, [in terms of] Adelaide, you'd be looking like your Finger Lickin' Goods. Like an example for me, when I saw Finger Lickin' Good on the Def Wish Cast album and just sort of started sinking things together as well. There's a sort of first posse cut, especially Australian posse cut that I'd heard.' Influenced by these early 1990s acts, more Hip-Hop artists began to emerge in Adelaide. According to a history of Hip-Hop published in street press magazine *Twenty4Seven* written by Madcap aka Derek Downing (2006: 11), there was a lull in Hip-Hop events in 1993. As a result, people began congregating in Blackwood at an infamous roundabout where they would rhyme (Downing

2006: 11). Regulars at these events included Flak, Delta, Madcap, Quro and 'young MCs named M-A-Double-T, Base T and Calli-C' who would become 'Suffa, Pressure and DJ Sum-1' (Downing 2006: 11). Over time, some of these acts coalesced into the Certified Wise collective.

Forming the posse: Certified Wise

One of the final tracks on *The Calling* is the posse track 'The Certificate' which is listed on the CD as featuring Certified Wise. This shorthand was necessary because the track features a slew of artists: the Hilltop Hoods themselves (Suffa, Pressure, Debris), members of After Hours (Edits, Headlock, Integer1/ Artistik Intalekt) members of the Funkoars (Hons, Sesta, Trials, DJ Reflux), members of Terra Firma (Simplex, Mic Lez, DJ Dyems), Flak aka Fatface from Cross Bred Mongrels, Blockade[1], Kolaps, the Expressionist, Trauma and DJ Snair.[2] According to Flak, Certified Wise began with: 'me, Debris and Flee. They were the first three members.' He said that the crew emerged out of the *Culture of Kings* compilation: 'Terra Firma were just formulating, coming together. Dymesy [DJ Dyems] came on the scene. We came up with an idea of putting together a compilation. The *Culture of Kings* compilation came first, and obviously a posse track came second, and then Certified Wise came third. So out of the *Culture of Kings* compilation came

---

[1] Sometimes written as Blokade.
[2] DJ Snair has appeared on some Cross Bred Mongrels releases but not all. Over the years he has been a part of many Hip-Hop crews and has been a live DJ for others. Most recently, he has been touring with the group Social Change.

Certified Wise' (The Lesson w/DJ Sanchez 2017b). The posse track that Flak is referring to here is called '13 MCs and 3 DJs' by Certified Wise on *Culture of Kings* (2000). It features all the above artists, except the members of the Funkoars, Mic Lez, the Expressionist and DJ Snair. It includes Flee and Raph AL who are not on 'The Certificate'. While Certified Wise were not the only Hip-Hop collective in Adelaide, they were a large group and were very prominent during the 2000s. Their visibility was boosted by performances on *Culture of Kings* and *The Calling* itself. In the next section, I provide some details about how 'The Certificate' was created.

Producing and recording 'The Certificate'

The MCs on 'The Certificate' were rhyming over the only beat on *The Calling* not produced by the Hilltop Hoods – a joint made by Dazastah from the Perth Hip-Hop group Downsyde and Syllabolix. Daz equated Syllabolix to Perth's Certified Wise. He told me that the Hilltop Hoods had performed in Perth prior to *The Calling*, although he could not recall specific details. He described having a 'chat with Suffa' who was planning 'The Certificate' and who asked him to 'send me something': 'I sort of made this quick loop cause Suffa was like 'oh I need something quick'. And I sent it to him. And he's like, 'yeah, that's dope'. Dazastah was planning to work on the track more, but this did not happen because of time constraints: 'I was meant to then develop it more and give him proper stems […] But he just used MP3 loop with a beat and chopped it up [laughs] So I was like, "I wanted to do some extra stuff to it man!" But I knew it was time sensitive.'

Like the rest of *The Calling*, 'The Certificate' was recorded at Debris' studio. Reflecting the importance of his early work in Cross Bred Mongrels with Flak, for a long period of time DJ Debris' studio and production was named after the group: X-Bred Production Studios. Raph AL described the vibe of the day:

> The whole crew was there […] it was just a good atmosphere. Debris' house was just fun like that, because you had the sort of the back room where he was in with all the music and so forth. Then the actual recording booth was inside the house where the backroom was just sort of separated from the main house […]. And in the backyard, the party was happening. So, it was basically just a massive party where individually people would sneak into the room, drop a verse and then come back to the party.

Frustratingly for Raph, even though he recorded a verse for 'The Certificate' it was ultimately cut. At the time of the recording session, he was living in Melbourne but happened to be in Adelaide. He wrote and recorded a verse in one hour but fellow Terra Firma member Simplex thought that it could be improved: 'Simplex goes "oh I reckon you could do better than that verse Raphy" and they deleted my verse. And then there's "oh we'll record it again for you" and this never happened.' Despite his verse being cut, Raph AL still has much respect for Certified Wise. He said that he still considers himself to be part of the collective and sees the other members as family.

Raph also emphasized the key role that Debris' studio played in the 2000s Adelaide scene, with many groups recording there before they had their own set-ups. Raph AL described Debris as being 'ahead of the curve, especially when it comes to technology'. He explained that Terra Firma would record at Debris' studio any chance they got, until Simplex set up his own studio. The group even inherited old equipment from Debris when he upgraded. DJ Debris' access to recording technology and willingness to share his knowledge and time helped several artists to make the transition from 'bedroom' acts to recorded artists. More broadly, the increasing accessibility of studio equipment made producing Hip-Hop at home and achieving a more professional sound a reality:

> Technology's got a bit to do with it, everyone's becoming a lot more aware of sound engineering and things are really progressing quickly […] a few years back it was a lot harder to make yourself sound professional if you were working with an old reel-to-reel tape recorder, but now you can make a halfway decent record on a home computer.
>
> (DJ Debris in Cleveland 2005: 7)

Certified Wise never officially disbanded but to my knowledge the name was last used for the 2009 Cross Bred Mongrels album which was titled *Certified Wise*. This project included production by Debris and Chris Bass with most tracks featuring MCs Flak and Flee alongside DJ Snair and a range of guest artists. This was also the beginning of the Golden Era Records phase from 2008 to 2017, when the Hoods left Obese Records and created their own label. From 2013 to 2016, Golden Era released annual 'cyphers' on a free mixtape with accompanying film clips hosted on YouTube. A cypher or cipher is a Hip-Hop term for 'the circle of participants and onlookers that closes around battling rappers or dancers as they improvise for each other' (Chang 1997: 60). These improvisations are often called 'freestyles'. The Golden Era cyphers replicated some of the elements of an organic cypher that can emerge on the street, at parties, or at Hip-Hop events, like people taking turns to perform and 'one-up' each other. However, there was no audience interaction, and the performances were not freestyles. While no new cyphers have been released since 2017, they were so popular that people still talk about them and request new ones. These Golden Era cyphers could be seen as an extension of the early Certified Wise posse tracks, and like 'The Certificate' and other tracks on *The Calling*, they build on a long Hip-Hop tradition of competitive rhyming and battling.

Battle raps and beat box interludes: Competition and masculinity

> Hip-Hop has just always been hyper competitive. It's always been that way. So no matter what country what era, that's always going to exist, and it's a male dominated art form. And dudes in general, are just competitive. In my opinion, it's always been that way and it'll never change.

> (DJ Sanchez)

Like DJ Sanchez, many people both in Australia and around the world characterize Hip-Hop as an inherently competitive and masculine culture. When I asked DJ Sanchez about the origins of Hip-Hop, he defined Hip-Hop as a 'Black art form that originated in the Bronx', tracing its cultural origins back further to the game enslaved Africans and their descendants would play, called 'the Dozens'. In a chapter titled 'Lyrics and Flow in Rap Music', Oliver Kautny (2015) provides a concise overview of the role that different forms of duelling including the Dozens have played in Hip-Hop culture.[3] While the focus of this book has been music, battling to prove your excellence is part of all Hip-Hop Elements, taking place in both informal and formal competitions. Graffiti Writers fight for space and respect on the street, Breakers and DJs participate in judged competitions or vie for the biggest crowd reaction when they perform. The significance of these competitions in the mid-2000s was emphasized by Maya Jupiter: 'let's not forget about the DJ battles, the ITF [International Turntablist Federation], DMCs [Disco Mix Championships], that took place. It was such a movement, around turntablism. You had DJs, who were extremely technical and practised and won titles. And then we also had a lot of B-Boy, B-Girl competitions as well, where crews battled each other.' For MCs, impromptu cyphers and formalized MC Battles were a common testing ground.

When I conducted fieldwork for my PhD, freestyling in cyphers at events was common. Arrival at a Hip-Hop gig was often signalled by seeing and hearing a cypher in a nearby side street – a circle of people huddled in the cold night air, their bodies illuminated by streetlights, heads nodding along, hands punctuating the rhymes. I also went to several Hip-Hop shows that featured formal MC battles. These involved MCs signing up to compete and battling each other in a knock-out tournament that was judged by crowd reaction or a panel of

---

[3] For an extended discussion of the Dozens see the book *Talking 'Bout Your Mama* by Wald (2012). As the title of this book suggests, rhymes and insults used when playing the dozens and in Hip-Hop battles often centre on people's mothers. The international impact of these traditions can be seen in one of the early taglines for Obese Records – 'fatter than ya mama'. This is a play on the meaning of 'fat' or 'phat' which can also refer to Hip-Hop beats (see Maxwell 2003).

experts. Formal MC Battles had a long history in Australia but were reinvigorated when the semi-autobiographical movie *8 Mile* (2002) starring Eminem was released. At a battle event, a DJ would drop a beat and each person would have a set time to rap.[4] Rhymes were supposed to be made up on the spot but were sometimes pre-written. Having easily identifiable pre-written rhymes made you an easy target and it was important to respond to what the other MC was saying. The overall aim was to outwit and belittle your opponent.

For many people that I interviewed, this combative aspect of Hip-Hop was enjoyable and important. Dazastah said that he loved the competitive nature of Hip-Hop and that the Hoods were always 'levelling up' and being chased by other groups. Similarly, Tomahawk described witnessing a battle between Suffa and MC Hunter[5] on the 93.7 Perth radio show that Hunter hosted with DJ Armee: '[Hunter] went straight for Suffa live on the radio and Suffa went right back at him. From that moment, I knew that Suffa was the real deal. I had nothing but respect for him. I remember sitting right next to them both and losing it laughing.' As Tomahawk outlines here, battling was a central way that Hip-Hop practitioners won respect. At this time, it was common for battle MCs to gain status through lyrics and punchlines that drew on socially ingrained prejudices and stereotypes about women and gay people, especially gay men. From 2004 to 2010, I saw many men perform rhymes that sought to humiliate and emasculate

---

[4]   Acapella battles became popular later but this was after I had conducted my fieldwork.

[5]   Hunter aka Robert Hunter was a member of Syllabolix who sadly passed away from cancer in 2011. Several people paid respect to him in interviews.

their opponent by claiming to have slept with their girlfriend or mother. It was standard practice to refer to your rival using a slur for a gay man and to craft lyrical attacks that questioned their heterosexuality.

Tomahawk went on to say when discussing the battle between Hunter and Suffa: 'nothing was taboo'. This competitive ethos of the cypher or a battle rap ideology heavily shapes the rhymes on *The Calling*. This is unsurprising, given the centrality of freestyling in Hip-Hop culture and the known participation of Pressure and Suffa in these events. Reflecting this time period, lyrics that include insensitive depictions of women and 'masculine' stereotypes can also be found on *The Calling*. On the interlude 'Simmy and the Gravyspitter', Suffa raps over a beat-box performed by Simplex from Terra Firma. The verse is a fiery attack on a generalized opponent, a warning to any MC that tries to battle him:

> Leave you torn, you couldn't battle me with that lame rhyme
> You couldn't come hard with two women at the same time

In this couplet the word 'come' is a double entendre. It refers to both the MCs inability to cum hard, as in ejaculate, even if they were sleeping with two women at the same time, and, their failure to write a 'hard' rhyme that 'comes' for their opponent. The track also includes lines that link wearing gold to being gay which I believe is disparaging. Namely, being gay is positioned as a failure to attain a socially constructed standard of 'masculinity'. Across the album there are other lines that work in the same way, where 'femininity' and gayness are depicted as being 'soft' and denigrated, while 'hardness' is linked to masculinity and celebrated.[6] These gendered

---

[6]   For an extended discussion of these themes and gender in Adelaide Hip-Hop see Arthur (2010: 116–27).

discourses are not unique to Hip-Hop from Australia. In an article which explores how gender, sexuality and nationalism intersect in 1970–80s Australian rock music, Hawkings (2014: 3) identifies 'Oz Rock' as a 'space within which the "script" of a hyper-heteromasculine national identity was reiterated and reconstructed'.[7]

I asked most people that I interviewed if there were any themes or lyrics on the album that were dated or had not aged well. Many responded that it was difficult for them to remember specific examples, so in hindsight it would have been better to ask direct questions about the representation of gay men and women on the album using examples. My findings are also limited because I asked people about their gender but not their sexual orientation. There is a pressing need for more Hip-Hop research in Australia written by and centring the experiences of LGBTIQ+ people. This is work that is being done by journalists like Kish Lal including a two-part profile of 'Black women and Black non-binary' Hip-Hop artists. In Part One, Miss Blanks says: 'I find it really problematic when I hear white cis male rappers spew blatant sexism and misogyny [while] flexing their entitlement and privilege on a daily basis like it's a car running out of fuel' (Lal n.d.).

In terms of *The Calling* specifically, some people that I interviewed said that there were lines on the album that they thought were homophobic or misogynistic. They indicated that while this was common in the broader Hip-Hop scene at the time, it would no longer be acceptable. MITUS said that it was important to view lyrics on *The Calling* 'in the context

---

[7] Her work builds on Mosher and Sirkin's (1984 in Hawkings 2014: 2) discussion of hypermasculinity defined as '(a) callous sexual attitudes towards women, (b) violence as manly, and (c) danger as exciting'.

of the time [...] these guys when they were making this music were young kids. Now they're adults with kids of their own'. Similarly, Kultar Ahluwalia noted that misogyny and homophobia were 'littered throughout the scene at the time. That's not really an indictment on the Hoods per se, it's more just that was pervasive in the culture. And not just pervasive in the Australian Hip-Hop scene, but just in Hip-Hop culture in general.' Some people that I interviewed raised concerns about lyrics from the album being analysed out of context, stressing that during this period these battle rhymes were performed without malice and were intended to be playful. While I do not want to justify or minimize the impacts of lyrics which people may find offensive, from my perspective the lyrical content on *The Calling* is less explicit than many US, or even other Australian songs, released prior to and during this period.

I note here that I am speaking from my position as a heterosexual cisgender woman and am not claiming to represent the views of all Hip-Hop fans and artists. It should go without saying that people can interpret Hip-Hop tracks in diverse ways. For example, DJ Josie Styles identified 'Simmy and the Gravyspitter' as her favourite on the album and did not seem to be concerned about the lyrical content. She said that she was proud of this track because it drew attention to beat-boxing, a less visible part of the Hip-Hop scene in Australia: 'Oh, fucking Simmo [Simplex] killed it [...] It was an expression of the time, there was beat boxers, which were there was only like five beat boxers in Australia, you can name pretty much all of them and then there was rappers. [...] I'm really proud they put that on to be honest, I rate that track the most.'

Once again, this highlights the need for thoughtful considerations of how different people respond to Hip-Hop lyrics, and the relationship between lyrics and beats. Without speaking to the members of the Hilltop Hoods, it is impossible to know if and how their own understandings of these lyrics have changed over time. As I explore in the final section of this chapter, it seems that the Hoods and other artists are re-evaluating their earlier bodies of work.

Vice-signaling: Re-evaluations and possible regrets

Some of the most problematic lyrics on *The Calling* are found on 'The Certificate' posse track, including verses by the members of the Funkoars who were known for their self-described 'filthy' lyrics (Moskovitch 2014). Ben Iota noted that the Funkoars were 'influential and among numerous Hip-Hop groups that leaned into vice-signaling, which had a ripple effect Australia-wide'. I interpret Ben's use of the term 'vice-signaling' as meaning lyrics that discussed 'vices' like alcohol and drug use, sexual promiscuity, interactions with female fans and sex-workers. When asked about how their romantic partners responded to their lyrical content in a 2007 *Stealth* interview, Trials maintained that they knew it was 'just a joke' and that their rhymes were only 'half-truths' (Pollard 2007: 61). More recently, he seems to be regretful about some of their content: 'we were literally too young to get into the clubs and do the things that we were rapping about. We were 16 and 17 years old when we started putting these things on record that lasts forever' (Condon and Tran 2022).

Trials (Daniel Rankine) is a Ngarrindjeri man who is a highly respected producer as well as a talented MC. He is also half of the acclaimed group A.B.Original with Yorta Yorta MC Briggs (Adam Briggs). A.B.Original's 2016 album *Reclaim Australia* was a blistering and witty condemnation of the racist settler-state and a celebration of the strength of First Nations peoples. The involvement of Trials in both the Funkoars[8] and A.B.Original suggests the need for nuanced accounts of the diverse music that Hip-Hop artists create, and how their material can change over time. Interestingly, the Hoods themselves now seem to be revisiting and re-evaluating their earlier work. In August 2022, they released the single 'A Whole Day's Night' featuring vocalist Montaigne who identifies as a 'queer woman of colour' (Jane 2020) and beat-boxer Tom Thum. In their official newsletter (Hilltop Hoods Newsletter 2022) they wrote: "'A Whole Day's Night" is a response to our own song, 'What a Great Night'. It's a reflection on how we look at the same situation 15 years later. How what we considered a celebration back in the day, could be considered a regret in the present'. 'What a Great Night' is a song from the album *The Hard Road* (2006). It celebrates a rowdy night of drunken fighting and Graffiti Writing, whereas the updated track highlights the negatives of out-of-control drinking. This includes inadvertently offending people, not being able to remember what you did and suffering from a hang over the next day.

As I explore in the conclusion to this book, the music that the Hoods release in 2022 and their lyrical themes are very different to *The Calling* era. They seem to be less influenced by

---

[8]   A new Funkoars album was rumoured for several years in the 2010s but it appears that the group are no longer active.

the competitive boasting of 2000s battle rap and more aware of the possible negative impacts of their messages, puns and language choices. In this final chapter, I also highlight other changes that have occurred in 'Australian' Hip-Hop since the 2000s and sum up the overall significance of *The Calling* as a 'pivot point' (Dazastah) in the Australian scene.

8 Conclusion – 'The Sentinel'

That's it. That is number one [...] The Calling is so polished sonically, and the impact that it had for the game, for the culture, for the scene. There's just nothing. There's just nothing that compares to it.

(DJ Sanchez)

That album was the quintessential becoming of Australian Hip-Hop that announced Australian Hip-Hop was to be taken seriously.

(MITUS)

It just elevated the quality of what Hip-Hop could be in this country. There'd been little sprinklings of commercial success, and wider mainstream success, prior to The Calling but The Calling sort of smashed all of that out of the park [... it] became the benchmark that people were aiming towards.

(Kultar Ahluwalia)

The bonus track on *The Calling*, 'The Sentinel' tells the story of a Hip-Hop group who stumble into a pub that initially seems inviting, only to find that they are now stuck there forever. It is a reference to the title track 'Hotel California' from the Eagles album released in 1976. This inspiration has been discussed by Suffa, who said that he grew up listening to 'Hotel California' being played by his parents (*The Calling Live* 2005). The Hilltop Hoods' iteration involves the group coming across a pub called

The Sentinel which is serving cheap beer and playing dope Hip-Hop tunes. At first, everything seems great but slowly they start to notice strange things about the clientele. Suffa and Pressure enter an MC Battle which keeps going on and on. When they try to leave the stage:

> The manager said, 'You boys can never leave this tournament
> And you can never leave the Sentinel', and the chorus went

The chorus of the song is a catchy 'ba ba ba ba ba' which even when typed out will probably immediately play in the heads of anyone who is familiar with it. This song was identified as a favourite track by both MITUS and Kultar Ahluwalia who said that they enjoyed the storytelling aspect of it.

Unlike the characters in 'The Sentinel', the story of the Hilltop Hoods is not over. They are not caught in a loop, doomed to forever repeat the past. They continue to experiment with their sound, to release new music and tour to sell-out audiences. The break-out success of *The Calling* enabled them to quit their jobs and focus on music full-time. As I explore in this final chapter, since this initial breakthrough a lot has changed for both the Hoods and other Hip-Hop artists in Australia.

From indie to major: Obese to Golden Era and beyond

Since the success of *The Calling*, many Hip-Hop fans have been happy about the recognition and respect that Hip-Hop has gained in Australia and the new opportunities that have been emerging for other artists. That said, there has also been a level of suspicion and scepticism about what these changes might mean for a formerly underground scene. For the Hoods, this suspicion manifested in their new music being scrutinized by Hip-Hop fans and other artists who were looking for evidence that they had 'sold out'. This scrutiny is the toxic flipside of the positive aspects of community. Community expectations can become a millstone around the necks of Hip-Hop artists who find themselves trying to protect Hip-Hop culture, remaining loyal to the underground. The impetus that the Hoods may have felt to 'keep it underground' can be seen in a 2012 interview promoting their album *Drinking from the Sun*. Suffa describes the album as 'basically a statement about underground hip hop culture coming up into the light […] we'll never forget where we came from and we still consider ourselves ambassadors for the hip hop underground' (The Music 2012).

In the same interview, Pressure states that many fans did not react well to the group's success: 'it's like when Nosebleed Section really broke for us; you had a small minority of the underground heads […] who were quick to call us sell-outs. But they came around because they saw that we were sticking to our guns and that other local artists were blowing up as well'. Here, being underground is positioned as an ideology that can be maintained *alongside* increasing popularity so long as artists are able to 'stick to their guns'. To this day, the Hoods still reference their connection to the underground in their promotional material, such as their 2022 biography which describes them as 'trailblazers in a genre that eventually married the underground with commercial success' (Hilltop Hoods Website, Biography n.d.). Cynically this could be viewed as a marketing tactic designed to appeal to underground Hip-Hop fans but given the dramatic expansion of the Hoods' audience this might not be the case.

In Chapter 6, I showed that many Hip-Hop practitioners were suspicious about the motivations of major record labels when *The Calling* was released. They questioned the ability of these corporations to understand Hip-Hop culture and were concerned that artists who signed with them would lose creative control. In this context, the fact that Obese Records were an independent label run by people from the scene itself contributed to the Hoods' success. Over time these fears about the influence of major labels began to lessen and ultimately the Hoods left Obese for their own label Golden Era. I do not know why they made this decision; it is a story that only they or Pegz can share from their own perspectives. As far as I am aware, Golden Era is a subsidiary of Island Records Australia/ Universal Music Australia which is part of the broader Universal Music Group.

The Hoods released three albums through Golden Era (*State of the Art* 2009; *Drinking from the Sun* 2012; *Walking Under the Stars* 2014). In 2017, they announced that they were stepping back from the label so that they could 'focus on our children and our music' (Newstead 2017). During the Hoods' tenure, Golden Era released a number of albums and EPs from A.B.Original's (*Reclaim Australia* 2016)[1] to Vents (*Marked for Death* 2011). Since 2017, Golden Era has been run by former operations manager Ben Martin who is also the Marketing and A&R Manager for Universal Music Australia. The Hoods have continued their relationship with Island Records Australia/ Universal Music Australia, and they are listed as 'Artists' on the Island Records website.

---

[1] This was a joint release with Bad Apples Music, a label and distributor formed by Briggs to promote Aboriginal and Torres Strait Islander artists.

In addition to changing record labels, the Hoods sound and style has also developed. This has included a shift from a rawer 1990s sample-based sound to the increased use of live instrumentation and singing alongside rapping. From Pressure's perspective, these developments are just part of the creative process and reflect changes in their lives: 'I don't want to make the same music I was making 20 years ago […] we made angry and grimy music back then and that's not who I am anymore. I'm 20 years older and a father' (Tokatly 2019). These changes have not been welcomed by all members of their fanbase. Indeed, some people that I interviewed said that they preferred the Hoods' music pre-*The Calling*. Some artists were also frustrated by groups who emerged after the Hoods and seemed to be emulating their style: 'absolute rinse and repeat of the Hoods. You know, there were so many people just copying, copying in a genre that copying is not okay' (Beats). Here Beats is talking about the rejection of 'biting', copying someone else's style, that emerged from Graffiti Writing but is shared across all Hip-Hop Elements. Beats thought the success of the Hoods resulted in people 'making songs intentionally to go on the radio' and that 'money ruins everything'.

While these kinds of fears about the corrupting influence of money were prominent in the 2000s, some people looked back on this ideology with regrets: 'there was this big thing of not selling out. It was almost to a detriment […] "Nah, I'm not doing that because I'm not selling out". […] It was ridiculous' (MITUS). These concerns about the dangers of the purist 'keep it real' mentality were reflected in broader evaluations of Hip-Hop in Australia that emerged in the 2010s. While many people looked back on the 2000s as a period of community support and growth, others thought Hip-Hop was being shaped in unhealthy ways by the struggle to legitimize it. As

Hip-Hop artist Seth Sentry said in an interview: 'Australian hip hop is definitely a grassroots movement, and I think supporting one another is an important aspect of it. I just feel as though we were too caught up in that whole thing for a while. It kind of held us back a bit' (Young and John 2017). As I explore below, as Hip-Hop in Australia became more accepted by the mainstream media, music industry and the public, Hip-Hop practitioners began to evaluate its past and think critically about its future. This included fears that white nationalism and racism were becoming issues in the scene.

'Aussie Hip-Hop' and white nationalism: Rejecting racism

So far, I have used terms like 'community' or 'scene' unproblematically, but it should be stressed that who/what comprises the 'scene' and if it is even possible to talk about a national 'Australian Hip-Hop community' cannot be assumed. Any consideration of Hip-Hop in Australia must examine how ideas about the nation or community are both constructed and contested through Hip-Hop practices. In Australia, as around the world, participation in Hip-Hop culture is a means for people to form and negotiate their identities. For many, it is a potent medium for political resistance and expression. For First Nations peoples and culturally and linguistically diverse (CALD) communities,[2] this has included powerful critiques

---

[2] I note concerns raised by some academics that the term culturally and linguistically diverse (CALD) perpetuates the othering of non-white people in Australia.

of the settler-state and the ongoing impacts of colonization (Kelly and Clapham 2019; Saunders 2020). Kelly and Clapham (2019: 159) write that in Australia, Aboriginal Hip-Hop practitioners have created their own 'parallel tradition' which 'engages with the wider Australian scene on its own terms'. In our interview, Maya Jupiter discussed her first encounter with this 'parallel tradition' when she went to an Aboriginal Hip-Hop event in Sydney and realized that there was a vibrant 'scene' or 'community' happening that she had been unaware of: 'it's a Hip-Hop night full of Indigenous MCs, Aboriginal MCs, and Aboriginal community showing up'.

Similarly, DJ Sanchez said that when he first started to discover local Hip-Hop it was very 'white dominated' and that this surprised him as a person who was born in Latin America and came from an 'American rap background, which is predominantly Black'. He explained that because of this history he 'was wondering, 'where are the Aboriginal rappers at?'. Over time he became aware that First Nations people were actively creating Hip-Hop, but as Maya Jupiter described, these practices often took place in sovereign, community-run spaces. Maya told me that it was imperative to recognize that Aboriginal artists 'have been participating in Hip Hop since the early days' and do not receive 'as much attention or acknowledgement as they should'. This lack of recognition has meant that until recently (2010s onwards) the contributions of Hip-Hop practitioners from both First Nations and CALD communities have been under-represented in the Australian mainstream media.

The mid-2000s was also an era when people did not always speak publicly about their cultural backgrounds. For example, Daz from Downsyde said that he thought the scene had always been culturally diverse: 'Look at Funkoars, look at us

[Downsyde]' but that people's skills rather than their race or cultural background were the focus. This makes any argument about the increasing diversification of Hip-Hop over time too simplistic. It would be more accurate to say that while First Nations and CALD artists have always been active, in the past they were less likely to reap commercial rewards for their hard work.[3] Indeed, from the mid-2000s onwards, commercially successful Hip-Hop in Australia became increasingly 'synonymous with white "true blue Aussie" hip-hop' (Jenke 2020/2021). According to Ben Iota, during this period radio stations would often favour Australian artists who drew on tropes that reflected a 'confined version of Australian identity' via 'beer and barbeque rap'. He explained that for a time period before, during and after the Hoods' success, commercial radio stations were 'animated by local Hip-Hop that had this novelty factor for them'. Here it is important to note that while the mainstream success of the Hilltop Hoods created new business avenues for some artists, their sound and image also became a template that shaped how music industry professionals defined Hip-Hop in Australia.

Alongside the standardization of 'radio-friendly' Hip-Hop, efforts to legitimize and promote Hip-Hop created by Australians started to have unintended consequences as new fans connected with these nationalistic sentiments and began solely listening to local Hip-Hop. This practice was dismissed by many Hip-Hop artists that I interviewed for my PhD thesis who were worried that people were missing out on amazing

---

[3] This is not to suggest that no First Nations and CALD Hip-Hop artists were successful during this period but rather that they were not the majority and that they were not typically publicly celebrated for their achievements.

music from outside Australia. More importantly, they were concerned that newer fans did not respect the Black origins of Hip-Hop (Rodger 2019). The fanbase was perceived as splintering away from the 'conscious' politics that had defined underground Hip-Hop and towards a parochial nationalism that was appealing to racist or xenophobic listeners.

In 2012, these issues were brought to the fore when Thomas Rock, a later Def Wish Cast affiliate / member, went on the triple j Hip-Hop show and said that Hip-Hop was now 'attracting people that have that lean towards the white pride and white power thing which has no place in Hip-Hop whatsoever'. Subsequently, *The Vine* magazine wrote a story titled 'Does Aussie Hip-Hop Have a Problem with Racism?' that featured interviews with fourteen Hip-Hop artists.[4] In the article, Suffa said that he agreed there was an issue with racism amongst local Hip-Hop fans and this was part of the motivation for their 2012 track 'Speaking in Tongues' (*Drinking from the Sun*) which featured Chali 2na from US Hip-Hop group Jurassic 5. In the song, Chali 2na raps:

Biting the hand that created the platform
Attaching pseudo patriotic crap to a rap song

I interpret these lyrics as being a rejection of ignorant Australian Hip-Hop fans whose parochial nationalism should not be a part of Hip-Hop culture.

In the *Vine Magazine* interview, Suffa said that the Hoods were confused by the xenophobic beliefs of some fans because they did not align with the Hip-Hop music that had inspired them,

---

4   This series of events is discussed in Cox (2016); Kelly and Clapham (2019) and Rodger (2019). The original Vine article is no longer available online and I referred to a print copy for this book.

including politically charged music created by Black groups: 'we'd noticed some xenophobia in our fan base through the social networks. Which was confusing to us, because we'd been raised on everything from Public Enemy to Poor Righteous Teachers'. He went on to say that he thought these ideas had emerged from the struggle for Australian Hip-Hop to be accepted. While this sentiment 'came from a good place where we were trying to find our own identity', he was disappointed that it had turned into 'being overtly patriotic without cause'. He also flagged that their video for 'Rattling the Keys to the Kingdom' (Hilltop Hoods 2012) was designed to help platform other Hip-Hop artists who did not have significant commercial success in Australia: 'The people having success – us, Drapht, Bliss n Eso, 360 – there's not a lot of diversity there'.[5] This video featured Hip-Hop artists from across Australia and Tomahawk who is featured in the clip said 'they invited all of us to show love to us for all we have done for the culture'.

From 2012 onwards, media stories about Hip-Hop in this country have increasingly featured a much broader spectrum of artists than the acts mentioned by Suffa above. DJ Josie Styles said that this increasing representation was a step forward but still 'not as much' as she wanted to see: 'you've got like, Neo Soul […] people, like B Wise coming through, really big African influence, […] there's been a little more Aboriginal inclusion.

---

[5] Across their career, the Hoods have used their profile to platform other artists, most recently featuring A.B.Original and Adelaide-based Hip-Hop, Soul and RnB artist Elsy Wameyo as the supports on their national tour. From 2005 to 2017 they also ran a development initiative for South Australian and later Hip-Hop artists from across Australia called 'The Hilltop Hoods Initiative'. Winners received financial assistance and other prizes including mentoring.

Obviously, Briggs was probably the first to smash that. Yeah. Shout out to Briggs and Trials [A.B. Original]'. In a 2022 history of Australian Hip-Hop for Apple Music, Hau Latukefu said that the commercial dominance of white Hip-Hop artists resulted in First Nations artists and people from immigrant backgrounds creating 'their own pockets' (Apple Music 2022). Hau is a respected Hip-Hop artist who was born in Australia to Tongan parents. He was a member of Koolism, the host of the triple j Hip-Hop show from 2008 to 2022, and recently launched a record label with Sony Music Entertainment Australia called 'Forever Ever Records'. Hau indicated that overtime, the stories and experiences of First Nations Hip-Hop artists and people from immigrant backgrounds were increasingly 'being seen and heard' and that this 'had to happen [...] it was the breath of fresh air that Australia needed' (Apple Music 2022).

Despite these shifts, further structural changes in the music industry are needed to ensure that commercially successful Hip-Hop artists from Australia are not predominantly white men. Recently, MC Michael Craig, who is of mixed Sri Lankan and Italian descent, said when he started out in the industry in 2016: 'blonde-haired and blue-eyed white boys' were the acts that were being signed by labels (Aran 2021). He indicated that this was changing, particularly after the success of Sampa the Great.[6] However, he was suspicious of a surface-level

---

[6] Sampa the Great is a Zambian Hip-Hop artist raised in Botswana who lived in Australia from 2014 to 2020 and achieved significant success with her 2017 release *Birds and the BEE9* which won the Australian music prize. In her official biography, Sampa questions how the Australian media narrative about her shifted as she became more successful in Australia and overseas: 'Sampa The Great soon graduated from being "Zambian-born, Botswana-raised, Australia-based" to being "Australia's own" and "Zambian-Australian"; the latter of which were simply untrue' (Sampa the Great website, About n.d.).

industry interest in diversity as a marketing strategy used to commodify and package difference. He stated that he would like to see further changes at the decision-making level of the music industry: 'when more women of colour, and people from First Nations and African backgrounds are making decisions at the major labels, then I will accept that the industry has done a 180 over the last decade' (Aran 2021). As I discuss in the next section, while more women are now participating in Hip-Hop culture, numerous barriers remain.

Rooms of men: Changing gender dynamics

When I asked people about how the Hip-Hop scene in Australia had changed since *The Calling* era, several people mentioned that Hip-Hop was not as male-dominated. This shift was also identified by Suffa in a recent interview where he said that early shows were 'just room after room of men' (Betoota Advocate Podcast 2022). Similarly, Ben Iota described late 1990s Adelaide Hip-Hop shows as being 'male-centric' but indicated that this started to shift in the mid-2000s. While noting that he might be viewing these early gigs through a specific lens as a seventeen-year-old man, he thought shows in the 1990s were 'menacing' and that this was because 'Hip-Hop promoted fierce competition, battling, crew rivalry' which meant that physical violence 'was present on people's minds'. He described 1990s audiences as being 'a real alcohol fueled crowd, you know, it was a lot of Writers. A lot of Graffiti Writers. That was probably the core group of people. It was very few women there.' In his opinion by the 2000s Hip-Hop events were more professional, less hostile and attracted more female Hip-Hop fans and practitioners. These descriptions also accord with my own experiences at Adelaide Hip-Hop gigs from roughly 2004 onwards, with a heavier period of participation from 2006 to 2008. Although men were the clear majority at these events, I noticed an increase in women's participation over time and I did not witness any physical violence.

In interviews for this book, Maya Jupiter, Josie Styles and Layla spoke about their experiences as women in this male-dominated culture, which was described by Josie as a 'patriarchal subculture'. Josie went on to explain that the higher number of men participating in the scene was not 'limited to Australia' but was strange because Hip-Hop culture was 'quite homophobic'. Layla was grateful for 'not being excessively ridiculed for being female' and wanted to be judged on her 'skill level rather than being 'good for a girl'. She highlighted the therapeutic power of Hip-Hop, explaining that she wrote music to 'say what I needed to express and get off my chest in order to heal'. Maya described being bullied on message boards and harassed at shows. She was in her twenties when this was occurring, and she found it challenging to navigate her femininity in a context where her body and practices were frequently being judged. For example, she was once criticized for 'moving her hips' when she performed. Her song 'The Truth' (*Today* 2003) was a response to this: 'I'm much more than my hips. I've got a lot to say'. While Maya touched on some of the challenging experiences that she had to navigate as a female MC, she also spoke powerfully about the joy that she got from her participation in a community of like-minded Hip-Hop practitioners. In the same way, Josie spoke about how she tried to use her platform to 'make a space for women […] a space for inclusion'. She used her position as a DJ, radio host and the only female employee at Sydney Hip-Hop store Next Level Records to mentor and support other women.

While they didn't necessarily choose these positions, artists like Maya, Josie and Layla are important role models for a new generation of female Hip-Hop artists, who still face significant challenges in the music industry. A recent independent review of the contemporary Australian music industry found 'unacceptable levels of sexual harm, sexual harassment and systemic discrimination' (Support Act Limited 2022: 2). Significantly, women and diverse, marginalized groups – in this report defined as First Nations peoples, People of Colour, people with a disability and LGBTIQ+ people – were more likely than men to experience sexual harassment and bullying. Clearly, there is much more work to be done, not solely in Hip-Hop culture but in the music field and Australian society at large. As Maya Jupiter poetically put it, Hip-Hop is no 'utopia', it mirrors broader social norms and beliefs: 'Hip hop is a reflection of our society, it will always be a reflection of who we are.' This is not to suggest that Hip-Hip cannot be a potent medium for protest, social justice and change – but rather that it should not become a scapegoat for racism, sexism and discrimination. Maya's hopes for the future of Hip-Hop were bound up in its ability to be 'a vehicle, to be a voice for those that are not given a large platform to speak out on'. She wanted Hip-Hop to continue to be a medium: 'to tell stories from Indigenous Australians, refugee Australians, culturally and linguistically diverse Australians, everyone that makes up what Australia truly is today, I hope that Hip-Hop continues to be that beautiful megaphone that allows us to continue to tell our stories, express ourselves and make a real positive change in our society'.

As highlighted above, the stories, labour and talent of Hip-Hop artists from diverse cultural backgrounds are increasingly being recognized in Australia. Hip-Hop artist Kaylah Truth,[7] reported that there had also been a shift in the Hip-Hop sound as a new generation emerged who were more open to experimentation: 'the beauty of the new wave of artists is that there seems to be an appreciation for those that don't box themselves in' (Young and John 2017). As I discuss below, this newfound sonic freedom was also highlighted by several people that I interviewed.

The legacy: New generations and creative freedoms

Now nearly twenty years after the release of *The Calling* in 2022, the Hoods are pursuing new ventures like a graphic novel. This novel is titled *Noctis* and is illustrated by Jeff Nice and written by Scott Dooley, Andrew Archer and the Hilltop Hoods. It will see the Hoods battle 'demonic aliens from another dimension' on a space station (@Hilltop Hoods 2021). In my opinion, this is a creative endeavour that would not have happened in the mid-2000s, a period when there was a conservative streak in the Hip-Hop scene. For example, Mark Pollard explained that he featured the group Celsius on the first full colour issue of *Stealth* because he liked the eccentricity of their first album (*Celsius* 1999).[8] Celsius are a group consisting of Sereck from Def Wish

---

[7] Kaylah Truth is a Gurang and Ngugi Hip-Hop artist. In an article for *The Guardian* via IndigenousX she wrote 'I hope that my blak, bisexual, femme presence on stage, screen or on the ground may be the representation that a young sister sees and realises that she too has a place in this world' (Truth 2019).

[8] The group's second album *Kicking it to Hell n Back* was released in 2004.

Cast and Brass Knuckles, who now goes by Brass. Mark Pollard felt that the creativity of groups like Celsius was 'stamped out' of the scene. He was happy that newer generations of Hip-Hop fans and artists seemed to have more freedom:

> I think the new generation has a fluidity that we did not have. When I reflect, especially, the Australian Hip-Hop scene in the 1990s. To me, it was very male [...] in my head, I was aging out of it, which is just a ridiculous attitude towards age, but I remember going to a few gigs, and I was like, this feels a little fascist. You get like 200 guys with knee high socks, like yelling 'Four Elements, Four Elements'. [...] That to me is not healthy.

Likewise, DJ Sanchez said that one of the positive changes that he had witnessed was that people involved in Hip-Hop were becoming 'more open minded': 'back in the day [...] you had to do it a certain way or you were wack. That attitude has definitely changed' (DJ Sanchez). He saw the 'dilution' of a 'purist' attitude as a good thing because it enabled growth. While he didn't listen to newer music like Drill or Grime, he was happy to see the success of new artists like Western Sydney Pasifika group ONEFOUR[9]: 'all that's happening now, it has all spawned from Kool Herc in like 78' with his decks and his speakers, the essence of Hip-Hop, and look at what it's grown into now [...] the growth of this culture has been enormous. And so long as it just continues to grow. That's really all I hoped for'. This hope for continued growth was echoed across several interviews where people spoke passionately about the central role that Hip-Hop had played in their lives and their continued

---

[9]   For an extended discussion of the criminalization of ONEFOUR and a definition of Drill, see Lee et al. (2022).

love for making beats, writing rhymes and other aspects of Hip-Hop production. If I had to identify one recurrent theme that links both the album *The Calling* and the interviews that I have conducted with Hip-Hop fans and artists, it would be – love for Hip-Hop culture.

This love is now being passed down to new generations, including the children of dedicated Hilltop Hoods fans. As I have been finalizing this book, I have been checking comments on the Hilltop Hoods' social media feeds to see how their 2022 tour is being received and have noticed that many comments are from parents who brought their children to the show. This phenomenon was already apparent in 2012 when I went to the 'Stopping All Stages' tour and made some fieldnotes including noting the wide range of people in attendance – a man with a Ramones t-shirt and mohawk, young children wearing earmuffs to protect their hearing, middle-aged women drinking red wine from plastic cups.[10] The Hoods are now a multi-generational group with a diverse fan base. There are no signs of a drop in popularity and the Hoods continue to produce new music. At the time of writing, they are slated to release not one but two new albums in 2023. While the Hilltop Hoods pursue new ventures, nostalgia remains high amongst long-time fans who are already rallying for a celebratory twenty-year anniversary *Calling* tour.

Although the Hoods might prefer to look forward, the success of *The Calling* should be recognized as playing a key role in changing how Hip-Hop was perceived and practised in Australia. The Hilltop Hoods themselves have never claimed responsibility for this shift, instead seeing themselves as one

---

[10] Like all fieldnotes, these descriptions are subjective assessments of people's age and gender.

group amongst many who were lucky to blow up: 'we were one of the groups that were there at the beginning, with a lot of other groups [...] I think it was inevitable that a group was going to break through because hip hop was just becoming such a popular subculture ... the bubble had to burst' (Suffa in Vinall 2012). While it may have been inevitable that a Hip-Hop group from Australia would become the 'break through' act who gained popularity outside of the tight-knit Hip-Hop scene, it was the Hoods' hard work, professionalism and musical talent that earned them this position and has enabled them to continue their music career decades later.

References

@Hilltophoods (2017) Instagram Post. 'Today We Announce That We Have Stepped Down from @goldenerarecords, Both as Artists and Owners', 15 December. Available online: https://www.instagram.com/p/BctGK5tFzmQ/ (accessed 27 September 2022).

@Hilltophoods (2019) Twitter Post. 'I've Made the "It's a Swan" Thing Worse, Haven't I', 17 May. Available online: https://twitter.com/hilltophoods/status/1129228069502242817 (accessed 6 September 2022).

@Hilltophoods (2020) Facebook Post. 'Blown Away. Thanks for Making Us the Most Streamed Domestic Artists in Australia Two Years in a Row Guys', 3 December. Available online: https://www.facebook.com/permalink.php?story_fbid=10158393676416359&id=12671606358 (accessed 27 September 2022).

@HilltopHoods (2021) Instagram Post. 'Noctis', 7 May. Available online: https://www.instagram.com/p/COjCvCnHHsM/ (accessed 7 September 2022).

Apple Music (2022) 'I Want This to Be the Place': The History and Evolution of Australian Hip-Hop', Available online: https://apple.news/ALrzIq7XBSwi2f1uWeRtbcA (accessed 6 September 2022).

Aran, C. (2021) 'How Aussie Hip-Hop Lost Its Twang: An Interview with Rapper Matthew Craig', *South Asian Australians Representing Ideas*. Available online: https://saaricollective.com.au/culture/blog/how-aussie-hip-hop-lost-its-twang-an-interview-with-rapper-matthew-craig/ (accessed 6 September 2022).

Arthur, D. (2010) 'The Symbolic Consumption of Subcultures: An Ethnographic Study of the Australian Hip Hop Culture', PhD diss., The University of Adelaide, Adelaide.

Attfield, S. (2020) 'Curse ov Dialect, Wooden Tongues (2006)', in J. Stratton and J. Dale with T. Mitchell (eds), *An Anthology of Australian Albums: Critical Engagements*, 111–23, New York: Bloomsbury.

Bam05 (2016) 'Hilltop Hoods – Nosebleed Section', YouTube. Available online: https://www.youtube.com/watch?v=lqCyTM1bF6Q (accessed 10 August 2022).

Beat (2010) 'Obese Records 10 Year Anniversary: Block Party', Available online: https://beat.com.au/obese-records-10-year-anniversary-block-party/ (accessed 30 July 2022).

Beers, Beats & The Biz (2021) 'Ep. 87 – Steppin' without the Essentials Featuring Shaheen Waheed aka Shazlek One', Available online: https://soundcloud.com/beersbeatsthebiz/ep-87-steppin-without-the-essentials-featuring-shaheen-waheed-aka-shazlek-one (accessed 2 September 2022).

Bellanta, M. (2012) *Larrikins: A History*, Queensland: University of Queensland Press.

Betoota Advocate Podcast (2022) '++Ep 224: The Hilltop Hoods', Available online: https://podcasts.apple.com/au/podcast/ep-224-the-hilltop-hoods/id1350346878?i=1000577596731 (accessed 19 September).

Bradley, A. (1999) 'Driven by the Sonic Language Passion', in G. Bloustein (ed) Musical Visions: Selected Conference Proceedings from 6th National Australian/New Zealand IASPM and Inaugural Arnhem Land Performance Conference, 21–2, South Australia: Wakefield Press.

Castiglia, A. (2016) 'Allday on Cracking America, Rapping Like an Aussie but Not Like a Bogan', *GQ*. Available online: https://www.

gq.com.au/entertainment/music/allday-on-cracking-america-rapping-like-an-aussie-but-not-like-a-bogan/news-story/fee0936cbc1e5e433523a5d4a7bd9783 (accessed 4 May 2022).

Census QuickStats (2021) 'South Australia', Available online: https://www.abs.gov.au/census/find-census-data/quickstats/2021/4 (accessed 6 September 2022).

Chalfant, H. and Prigoff, J. (1987) *Spray Can Art*, New York: Thames and Hudson.

Chang, J. (1997) 'It's a Hip-Hop World', *Foreign Policy*, November/December: 58–63.

Cleveland, S. (2005) 'Hoods "Rapped" in Hip-Hop Wave', *The Gold Coast Bulletin*, 20 January: 7.

Cobb, W. J. (2007) *To the Break of Dawn: A Freestyle on the Hip Hop Aesthetic*, New York: New York University Press.

Coby, B. (2009) 'Hilltop Hoods Interview: State of the Art', Access All Areas. Available online: https://web.archive.org/web/20090627183739/http://www.accessallareas.net.au/artists/Hilltop_Hoods.php (accessed 6 September 2022).

Colman, T. (2003) 'Boyz in the Hoods', *Sydney Morning Herald*, 7 November: 21.

Condon, D. and Tran, C. (2022) 'The Story of Trials', Double J. Available online: https://www.abc.net.au/doublej/music-reads/features/the-story-of-trials/13960206 (accessed 6 September 2022).

Cooper, M. and Chalfant, H. (1984) *Subway Art*, New York: Thames & Hudson.

Cox, J. (2016) 'It's Like DNA You Know?', Analysing Genealogies of Listening in Australian Hip Hop' Ph.D. diss., Macquarie University, Sydney.

Dart, C. (2012) 'Hilltop Hoods: Drinking from the Sun', *Exclaim!* Available online: https://exclaim.ca/music/article/hilltop_hoods-drinking_from_sun (accessed 4 August 2022).

Donovan, P. (2004) 'The New Beat on the Block', *The Age*, 9 September: 4.

Double J. (2017) 'Hilltop Hoods – The Calling', Available online: https://www.abc.net.au/doublej/programs/classic-albums/hilltop-hoods—the-calling/10273916 (accessed 30 April 2022).

Downing, D. (2006) 'The Concise History of Hip Hop in Adelaide: Part Two: The Nineties', *Twenty4Seven*, 16: 10–11.

D'Souza, M. and Iveson, K. (1999) 'Homies and Homebrewz: Hip Hop in Sydney', in R. White (ed) *Australian Youth Subcultures: On the Margins and in the Mainstream*, 55–64, Hobart: Australian Clearinghouse for Youth Studies.

Duffy, M. (2001) 'Hip-Hop Revival Turns Urban Style on Its Head', *The Advertiser*, 10 October: 34.

Dullroy, J. (2003) 'Last Friday Night the Alley Bar in Milton Witnessed the Surprise Hit Gig of the Year', *The Courier-Mail*, 7 November: 50.

Eberhardt, M. and Freeman, K. (2015) 'First Things First, I'm the Realest': Linguistic Appropriation, White Privilege, and the Hip-Hop Persona of Iggy Azalea', *Journal of Sociolinguistics*, 19(3): 303–27.

Edwards, P. (2009) *How to Rap: The Art and Science of the Hip-Hop MC*, Chicago: Chicago Review Press.

Eliezer, C. (2004) 'Hoods Down Under', *Billboard Magazine*, 21 August: 59.

Eliezer, C. (2018) 'Exclusive: Spotify Helps Hilltop Hoods Trace Their Musical Roots', The Music Network. Available online: https://themusicnetwork.com/exclusive-spotify-helps-hilltop-hoods-trace-their-musical-roots-being-able-to-work-with-some-of-our-influences-was-wild/ (accessed 6 May 2022).

Fiske, J. (2010) *Reading the Popular*, (Second Edition), New York: Routledge.

Fernandes, S. (2011) *Close to the Edge: In Search of the Global Hip Hop Generation*, London: Verso.

Frilingos, M. (2003) 'Reviews', *The Daily Telegraph*, 26 November: S26.

George, N. (2004) 'Hip-Hop's Founding Fathers Speak the Truth', in M. Forman and M. A. Neal (eds) *That's the Joint! Hip-Hop Studies Reader*, 45–55, New York: Routledge.

Girgis, L. (2019) 'The 10 best Hilltop Hoods Songs: Critic's Picks', Tone Deaf. Available online: https://tonedeaf.thebrag.com/the-10-best-hilltop-hoods-songs-critics-picks/ (accessed 1 August 2022).

Glicksman, J. (2021) 'The Kid LAROI Has the Streaming Numbers of a Superstar. Now He's Figuring Out How to Be One', Billboard. Available online: https://www.billboard.com/articles/columns/hip-hop/9551494/the-kid-laroi-streaming-numbers-debut-album-interview/ (accessed 5 May 2022).

Gougoulis, S. (2019) 'Hilltop Hoods Make History with Their Sixth #1 Album', triple j. Available online: https://www.abc.net.au/triplej/news/hilltop-hoods-make-history-with-their-sixth-no.1-album/10865504 (accessed 26 September 2022).

Gregson, D. (2004) 'It's Time to Talk Obese', *The Age*, 23 July: 18.

Hawkings, R. (2014) '"Sheilas and Pooftas": Hyper-Heteromasculinity in 1970s Australian Popular Music Cultures', *Limina*, 20(2): 1–14.

Hegarty, K. (2003) 'Rockin' the Party', *The Age*, 22 August: 17.

Hilltop Hoods (2007) 'Hilltop Hoods – Testimonial Year (Official Video)', YouTube. Available online: https://www.youtube.com/watch?v=yDx8nemwWgl (accessed 1 August 2022).

Hilltop Hoods (2012) 'Hilltop Hoods – Rattling the Keys to the Kingdom (Official Video)', YouTube. Available online: https://www.youtube.com/watch?v=Dr5SnlxIZCA (accessed 6 September 2022).

Hilltop Hoods (2022) 'Hilltop Hoods – The Nosebleed Section (Official Video)', YouTube. Available online: https://www.youtube.com/watch?v=Vak9wUPkL3Q (accessed 10 September 2022).

Hilltop Hoods Newsletter (2008) 'Golden Era Records', from <info@hilltophoods.com> received 8 August 2008.

Hilltop Hoods Newsletter (2022) 'LISTEN: New Single "A Whole Day's Night" + WIN: The Ultimate Hoods Prize Pack', from <info@au.umusic-online.com> received 25 August 2022.

Hilltop Hoods Website, 'Armageddon', (n.d.) Available online: https://hilltophoods.com/armageddon/ (accessed 30 July 2022).

Hilltop Hoods Website, 'Hilltop Hoods Biography', (n.d.) Available online: https://hilltophoods.com/biography/ (accessed 6 September 2022).

Hoad, C. and Gunn, R. (2019) 'Queer Contexts in Australia and Aotearoa/New Zealand', *Queer Studies in Media and Popular Culture*, 4(1): 3–12.

Jane, F. (2020) 'Montaigne Reflects on a Year of Creative Exploration', Star Observer. Available online: https://www.starobserver.com.au/artsentertainment/montaigne-reflects-on-a-year-of-creative-exploration/198427 (accessed 8 September 2022).

Jenke, B. (2020/2021) 'The 50 All Time Greatest Australian Hip-Hop Tracks', Available online: https://tonedeaf.thebrag.com/50-all-time-greatest-aussie-hip-hop-tracks' (accessed 10 August 2022).

Kautny, O. (2015) 'Lyrics and Flow in Rap Music', in J. A. Williams (ed) *The Cambridge Companion to Hip-Hop*, 101–17, Cambridge: Cambridge University Press.

Kelly, B. and Clapham, R. (2019) 'Decolonizing Aussie Hip Hop', in A. Hudson, A. Ibrahim and K. Recollet (eds) *In This Together: Blackness, Indigeneity, and Hip Hop*, 147–61, New York: DIO Press.

Laccarino, C. (2004) 'Fair Dinkum Hip-Hop Success', *Sun Herald*, 19 December: 24.

Lal, K. (n.d.) 'It's Time to Listen to More Diverse Voices in Australian Hip-Hop', Available online: https://acclaimmag.com/music/its-time-to-listen-to-more-diverse-voices-in-australian-hip-hop/#1 (accessed 19 September 2022).

Lal, K. (2019) 'History of Australian Hip-Hop in 19 Essential Tracks', Available online: https://junkee.com/longform/australian-hip-hop (accessed 16 April 2022).

Lee, M., Martin, T. Ravulo, J. & Simandjuntak, R. (2022) '[Dr]illing in the Name Of: The Criminalisation of Sydney Drill Group ONEFOUR', *Current Issues in Criminal Justice*, DOI: 10.1080/10345329.2022.2100131.

Maxwell, I. (2003) *Phat Beats. Dope Rhymes: Hip Hop Down Under Comin' Upper*, Middletown: Wesleyan University Press.

McMenemy, L. (2004a) 'Black Eyed Peas and Hoodoo Gurus – What a Day', *The Advertiser*, 30 January: 9.

McMenemy, L. (2004b) 'Hilltop Hoods Tour with Music Festival', *The Advertiser*, 11 November: 12.

McMenemy, L. (2005) 'Never Mind the Cold, Feel the Beat', *The Advertiser*, 5 February: 8.

McMenemy, L. (2006) 'The Road to Riches', *The Daily Telegraph*, 30 March: 50.

Minestrelli, C. (2016) *Australian Indigenous Hip Hop: The Politics of Culture, Identity and Spirituality*, New York: Routledge.

Mitchell, T. (1999) 'Another Root: Australian Hip Hop as a "Glocal" Subculture: Re-Territorialising Hip Hop', in G. Bloustein (ed) *Musical Visions: Selected Conference Proceedings from 6th National Australian/New Zealand IASPM and Inaugural Arnhem Land Performance Conference*, 85–94, South Australia: Wakefield Press.

Mitchell, T. (2001) 'Introduction: Another Root – Hip Hop outside the USA', in T. Mitchell (ed) *Global Noise: Rap and Hip Hop outside the USA*, 1–38, Middletown: Wesleyan University. Press, Middletown.

Mitchell, T. (2003) 'Indigenising Hip Hop: An Australian Migrant Youth Culture', in M. Butcher and M. Thomas (eds) *Ingenious: Emerging Youth Cultures in Urban Australia*, 198–214, North Melbourne: Pluto Press.

Mitchell, T. (2007) 'The DIY Habitus of Australian Hip Hop', *Media International Australia*, 123(1): 109–22.

Moreton-Robinson, A. (2015) *The White Possessive: Property, Power, and Indigenous Sovereignty*, Minneapolis: University of Minnesota Press.

Morrisey, T. (2014) 'The New Real: Iggy Azalea and the Reality Performance', *PORTAL*, 11(1): 1–17.

Moskovitch, G. (2014) 'Funkoars: "There's a Little More Method to the Madness This Time"', Available online: https://musicfeeds.com.au/features/funkoars-theres-a-little-more-method-to-the-madness-this-time/ (accessed 26 August 2022).

Murphy, K. (2004) 'Bias B: Keep It Movin', *Stealth Magazine*, 2(9): 68–71.

Newstead, A. (2017) 'Hilltop Hoods Part Ways with Golden Era Records ahead of New Album', triple j. Available online: https://www.abc.net.au/triplej/news/hilltop-hoods-part-ways-with-golden-era-records-before-new-album/9262570 (accessed 2 September 2022).

Obese Records Closing Down (2016) 'Reddit thread', Available online: https://www.reddit.com/r/AussieHipHop/comments/4gxsax/obese_records_closing_down/ (accessed 30 May 2022).

Obese Records Website, Biography (n.d.). Available online: http://obeserecords.com/obs/biography/ (accessed 30 July 2022).

O'Hanlon, R. (2006) 'Australian Hip Hop: A Sociolinguistic Investigation', *Australian Journal of Linguistics*, 26(2): 193–209.

Overell, C. (n.d.) 'Nation Unanimously Decides on Replacing Advance Australia Fair with the Nosebleed Section', Available online: https://www.betootaadvocate.com/headlines/nation-unanimously-decides-on-replacing-advance-australia-affair-with-the-nosebleed-section/ (accessed 10 September 2022).

Pennycook, A. and Mitchell, T. (2009) 'Hip Hop as Dusty Foot Philosophy: Engaging Locality', in H. S. Alim, A. Ibrahim and A. Pennycook (eds) *Global Linguistic Flows: Hip Hop Cultures, Youth Identities and the Politics of Language*, 25–42, New York: Routledge.

Point of Contact Festival (2022) 'Eventbrite', Available online: https://www.eventbrite.com.au/e/point-of-contact-adelaide-hip-hop-festival-10-day-pass-tickets-352113299357 (accessed 6 September 2022).

Pollard, M. (2004a) 'Skidmarks: An Editorial', *Stealth Magazine*, 2(9): 8.

Pollard, M. (2004b) 'DJ Peril: Speaking Japanese', *Stealth Magazine*, 2(8): 49–50.

Pollard, M. (2007) 'Funkoars: Staunch Raunch', *Stealth Magazine*, 14: 60–4.

Price-Styles, A. (2015) 'MC Origins: Rap and Spoken Word Poetry', in J. A. Williams (ed) *The Cambridge Companion to Hip-Hop*, 11–21, Cambridge: Cambridge University Press.

Rap News (2004) 'Obese Records: Bias B', Available online: https://rapnews.co.uk/?p=244 (accessed 30 August 2022).

Rodger, D. (2019) 'Forging Traditions: Continuity and Change in the mid 2000s Australian Hip-Hop Scene', *Ethnomusicology Forum*, 28(2): 217–40.

Rose, T. (1994) *Black Noise: Rap Music and Black Culture in Contemporary America*, Middletown: Wesleyan University Press.

Rule, D. (2008) 'Over the Hilltops, Still Far Away', *The Age*. Available online: http://www.theage.com.au/news/music/over-the-hilltops/2008/01/03/1198949965122.html?page=fullpage#contentSwap1 (accessed 30 August 2022).

Sampa the Great Website, About (n.d.). Available online: https://sampathegreat.com/about (accessed 6 September 2022).

Saunders, G. (2020) 'JustUS: What Hip-Hop Wants You to Know', PhD exegesis, University of Technology, Sydney.

Shaker, R. (2016) 'Exclusive: Rob Shaker Lists His Top 10 Australian Hip Hop Albums', OzHipHopShop. Available online: https://ozhiphopshop.com/australianhiphopnews/exclusive-rob-shaker-lists-his-top-10-australian-hip-hop-albums/ (accessed 10 August 2022).

Stealth Magazine (2004) '2003 Readers Poll Results', 2 (8):11.

Stratton, J. (2023) *Human Frailty*, New York: Bloomsbury.

Support Act Limited (2022) 'Raising Their Voices: Independent Review into Sexual Harm, Sexual Harassment, and Systemic Discrimination in the National Music Industry – Report Summary', Available online: https://drive.google.com/file/d/1R2oPxtvsNNlU8fD9JCCCnLspFdC7HLfq/view (accessed 7 September 2022).

Taylor, C. (2019) 'Interview with Hip-Hop Artist Matt Lambert of Hilltop Hoods', Available online: https://www.musicinminnesota.com/the-night-we-played-minneapolis-soundset-was-on-hilltop-hoods/ (accessed 5 August 2022).

The Advertiser (2003) 'The Week's Live Entertainment October 2–8', 2 October: 63.

The Advertiser (2005) 'Boys in the Hood', 8 January: W06.

The Lesson W/ DJ Sanchez (2017a) 'Fat Face Reflects on Hilltop Hoods "The Calling" Album Launch In Adelaide "It Was Just Nuts" (Pt. 3)', YouTube. Available online: https://www.youtube.com/watch?v=-dkSF1PulJ4 (accessed 10 August 2022).

The Lesson w/DJ Sanchez (2017b) 'Fat Face of Cross Bred Mongrels "Certified Wise Started with Me, DJ Debris & Flee" (Part 2)', YouTube. Available online: https://www.youtube.com/watch?v=dYp03O5umRw (accessed 6 September 2022).

The Music (2012) 'Sons of the Underground Arise', Available online: https://themusic.com.au/features/hilltop-hoods/EfUJBQQHBgk/18-03-12 (accessed 6 September 2022).

'The Nosebleed Section by Hilltop Hoods' (n.d.) National Film and Sound Archive of Australia. Available online: https://www.nfsa.gov.au/collection/curated/nosebleed-section-hilltop-hoods-0 (accessed 16 April 2022).

Tokatly, E. (2019) 'We Chat with Hilltop Hoods about The Great Expanse', *Blank*. Available online: https://blankgc.com.au/hilltop-hoods-the-great-expanse-interview/ (accessed 30 July 2022).

Tran, C. (2021) 'The J Files: Hilltop Hoods', Double J. Available online: https://www.abc.net.au/doublej/programs/the-j-files/hilltop-hoods-the-hard-road-clown-prince-nosebleed-section/13335128 (accessed 5 August 2022).

triple j (2019) 'Hilltop Hoods – "Leave Me Lonely" (Live for Like A Version)', YouTube. Available online: https://www.youtube.com/watch?v=38ikl0z429o (accessed 8 August 2022).

triple j (n.d.) 'Hottest 100: 20 Years', Available online: https://www.abc.net.au/triplej/hottest100/alltime/20years/countdown/ (accessed 6 September 2022).

Truth, K. (2019) 'I Hope My Blak, Bisexual, Femme Presence Shows a Sister That She Has a Place in This World', *The Guardian*. Available online: https://www.theguardian.com/commentisfree/2019/nov/28/i-hope-my-blak-bisexual-femme-presence-shows-a-sister-that-she-has-a-place-in-this-world (accessed 5 September 2022).

Tuskan, P. (2019) 'Hilltop Hoods Make Aussie Music History with 1 Million Album Sales', Available online: https://themusicnetwork.com/hilltop-hoods-million-albums/ (accessed 4 May 2022).

Vaughan, J. (2006) 'Boys from the Hood Take on the World', *The Advertiser*, 12 April: 9.

Vinall, F. (2012) 'Hilltop Hoods', Tone Deaf. Available online: https://web.archive.org/web/20170921023214/http://tonedeaf.com.au/hilltop-hoods-3/ (accessed 4 August 2022).

Vito, C. (2015) 'Who Said Hip-Hop Was Dead? The Politics of Hip-Hop Culture in Immortal Technique's Lyrics', *International Journal of Cultural Studies*, 18(4): 395–411.

Vito, C. (2019) *The Values of Independent Hip-Hop in the Post-Golden Era: Hip-Hop's Rebels*, Cham: Palgrave Macmillan.

Wald, E. (2012) *Talking 'Bout Your Mama: The Dozens, Snaps and the Deep Roots of Rap*, New York: Oxford University Press.

Wehner, C. (2006) 'Under the Hoods', *Herald Sun*, 30 March: L14.

Williams, J. A. (2015) 'Introduction: The Interdisciplinary World of Hip-Hop Studies', in J. A. Williams (ed) *The Cambridge Companion to Hip Hop*, 1–8, Cambridge: Cambridge University Press.

Yeaman, S. and McMenemy, L. (2005) 'Thirty Years of Rap, Rock, Hip-Hop and Shock', *The Advertiser*, 15 January: 46.

Young, A. J. and John, B. (2017) 'No More Gatekeepers: Examining the Changing Face of Aussie Hip Hop', Tone Deaf. Available online: https://tonedeaf.thebrag.com/examining-the-changing-face-of-aussie-hip-hop/list/early-days/ (accessed 6 September 2022).

Young, K. (2004) 'Rhyme of Their Lives', *The Mercury*, 1 July: 35.

Young, K. (2006) 'Hoods on Top of the World', *The Mercury*, 30 March: 27.

Zanfagna, C. (2015) 'Hip-Hop and Religion: From the Mosque to the Church', in J. A. Williams (ed) *The Cambridge Companion to Hip-Hop*, 71–84, Cambridge: Cambridge University Press.

Discography

A.B.Original (2016) *Reclaim Australia*, Golden Era Records/Bad Apples.

Adroit Effusive (2010) *Adroit Effusive: The Album*, Independent.

Brad Strut (2001) *The Authentic*, Obese Records.

Celsius (1999) *Celsius*, Basic Equipment.

Celsius (2004) *Kickin It to Hell N Back*, Crookneck Records.

Clandestien (2003) *Dynasty*, Independent.

Cross Bred Mongrels (2006) *Certified Wise*, Independent.

Def Wish Cast (1993) *Knights of the Underground Table*, Random Records.

Eagles (1976) *Hotel California*, Asylum Records.

Finger Lickin' Good (1993) *Illegitimate Sons of the Bastard Funk*, Illegitimate Records.

Layla (2005) *Heretik*, Obese Records.

Malcolm McLaren (1983) *Duck Rock*, Charisma Records.

Marley Marl (1988) *In Control, Volume 1*, Warner Bros. Records.

Maya Jupiter (2003) *Today*, Mother Tongues.

Melanie (1972) *Garden in the City*, Buddah Records.

Hilltop Hoods (1997) *Back Once Again* [EP], Independent.

Hilltop Hoods (1999) *A Matter of Time*, Independent.

Hilltop Hoods (2001) *Left Foot, Right Foot*, Independent.

Hilltop Hoods (2003) *The Calling*, Obese Records.

Hilltop Hoods (2006) *The Hard Road*, Obese Records.

Hilltop Hoods (2007) *The Hard Road: Restrung*, Obese Records.

Hilltop Hoods (2009) *State of the Art*, Golden Era Records.

Hilltop Hoods (2012) *Drinking from the Sun*, Golden Era Records.

Hilltop Hoods (2014) *Walking Under the Stars*, Golden Era Records.

Hilltop Hoods (2019) *The Great Expanse*, Universal Music Australia.

Reason (2000) *Solid*, Obese Records.

Sampa the Great (2017) *Birds and the Bee9*, Big Dada Recordings.

Various Artists (1999) *Rock Da City*, Nuffsaid Recordings.

Various Artists (2000) *Culture of Kings: The Australian Hip Hop Compilation*, Obese Records.

Various Artists (2002) *Culture of Kings: Volume Two*, Obese Records.

Various Artists (2002) *Obesecity*, Obese Records.

Various Artists (2003) *Culture of Kings: Three*, Obese Records.

Vents (2011) *Marked for Death*, Golden Era Records.

Filmography

8 Mile (2002) [Film] Dir. C. Hanson, US, Universal Pictures.

Beat Street (1984) [Film] Dir. S. Lathan, US, Orion Pictures.

Flash Dance (1983) [Film] Dir. A. Lyne, US, Paramount Pictures.

Hilltop Hoods (2005) [DVD] *The Calling Live*, AU, Obese Records.

Hilltop Hoods (2007) [DVD] *City of Light*, AU, Obese Records.

Style Wars (1983) [Film] Dir. T. Silver, US, Public Art Films/PBS.

Wild Style (1983) [Film] Dir. C. Ahearn, US, Rhino Home Video.

Index

Names of record albums and CDs are shown in italics, as in *The Calling*. Tracks/songs are enclosed in single quote marks. As main headings, they are followed by their performance group, enclosed in parentheses, as in 'The Sentinel' (Hilltop Hoods).

A

Aboriginal Hip-Hop (*See* First Nations Hip-Hop artists)

accents, local (*See* American vs local accents)

Ahluwalia, Kultar
    launch of *The Calling* 47
    misogyny and homophobia in Hip-Hop 80
    success of *The Calling* 85
    Thebarton Theatre performance 50

A Matter of Time 48

American vs local accents 13, 15

Armageddon 31–3

Australian Hip-Hop
    authenticity 13, 15, 16
    collaboration and positive relationships 59, 62, 65–6
    connections to international 62
    cultural appropriation 13–14
    discrimination 98
    distinctive art form 13, 14
    exclusion of non-Anglo Australians 14, 15
    history 12–14, 15, 59–62, 70–1, 95
    increasing diversity 94–5
    maintenance of counterculture 66–7, 87, 89–90
    male dominated culture 96, 97
    marginalised counterculture 59–61
    openness to innovation 99, 100
    retail outlets 18
    structural changes needed 95–6
    suspicion of major record labels 22, 64, 88
    valued independence 22–3, 63–4, 65
    white nationalism and racism 17, 93–4
    the word 'Australian' 16–17
    (*See also* Hip-Hop)

Australian Recording Industry Association (ARIA) awards 19

'A Whole Day's Night' (Hilltop Hoods) 82

B

Bass, Chris
- 'Australian' Hip-Hop 16–17
- Australian Hip-Hop as marginalised counterculture 59–60
- launch of *The Calling* 46

battle raps
- demoralising opponents 37, 69
- formal competitions 76–7
- gendered stereotypes 77–9

beat boxing 80

Beats
- contribution of *Culture of Kings* 62
- inappropriate copying of Hilltop Hoods 89
- launch of *The Calling* 35, 48
- Thebarton Theatre performance 50

Bellanta, Melissa 56–7

Betoota Advocate 40

Big Day Out festivals 51

Black Noise (book) (Rose) 11–12

Blaze 13

Bobbit, Ollie 17

Breaking in Australia 13, 14

C

Certified Wise
- Cross Bred Mongrels album 74
- origins 71

Craig, Michael 95–6

culturally and linguistically diverse (CALD) communities

commercial rewards 92

critiques of the settler-state 90–1

exclusion from Australian Hip-Hop 15

Culture of Kings
- emergence of Australian Hip-Hop community 62
- origins of Certified Wise 71–2

cyphers 74–5, 76

D

Dazastah
- beat for 'The Certificate' 72
- competitive Hip-Hop 77
- contribution of *Culture of Kings* 62

Debris, DJ 21
- music-making of Hilltop Hoods 42
- radio support for Hip-Hop 39
- recording studio 73, 74

'Decolonizing Aussie Hip Hop' (book chapter) (Kelly and Clapham) 14–15

Def Wish Cast 49

Drinking from the Sun 87

'Dumb Enough'
- 'It's a swan' 35–6
- wordplay critique of other groups 37

E

Easter egg references 27

Engelhardt, John 31, 32

Index

119

F

female Hip-Hop artists 97–8
First Nations Hip-Hop artists
   commercial rewards 92
   creating own settings 91, 95
   engagement with
      transnational anti-racism
      14
   pressure from 'Anglo' Hip-
      Hop 15–16
Flak (aka Fatface)
   launch of *The Calling* 47
   origins of Certified Wise 71
   Thebarton Theatre
      performance 49–50
Francis, Barry (*See* Debris, DJ)
Funkoars 81
Funnell, Ben
   Australian Hip-Hop
      as underground
      community 55
   Canberra launch of *The*
      Calling 52

G

Girgis, L 26
Golden Era Records 74, 75, 88
Graffiti Writers 13, 14, 96

H

Hawkings, R 79
Hilltop Hoods
   audience participation 38–9
   Big Day Out festivals 51
   diverse fan base 101
   early equipment 23–4
   effect on definition of
      Australian Hip-Hop 92

Golden Era Records 74, 88
   history 21–3, 25–6, 56,
      88
   live performances 38, 49–51,
      52
   management 22
   mutual relationship with
      Obese Records 19
   Noctis (book) 99
   re-evaluation of earlier work
      82, 83
   socio-political issues 55–6,
      57–8
   song structures 42–3
   stagecraft 38–9, 52
   support for Australian Hip
      Hop 94 n.5
Hip-Hop
   comparison with religious
      devotion 30
   as competitive performance
      75, 76, 77
   and construction of identity
      90
   Elements 11 n.1
   love for the culture 101
   and masculinity 78, 79
   origins 11–12, 75
   posse tracks 69–70
   required skills of MCs 38
   spread across North
      America 12
   underground
      counterculture 14, 63–4,
      87
Hip-Hop, Australian (*See*
      Australian Hip-Hop)
homophobia 77, 78

I

'Illusionary Lines' (Hilltop Hoods)
   commercialisation of Hip-
      Hop 64–5
   socio-political issues 58
Indigenous Hip-Hop (*See* First
   Nations Hip-Hop artists)
Iota, Ben
   Australian Hip-Hop
      development 28, 51
   contribution of *Hard Road* to
      Australian Hip-Hop 23
   contribution of *The Calling*
      to Australian Hip-Hop 19
   Hip-Hop as competitive 76
   influence of underground
      American Hip-Hop 63
   launch of *The Calling* 49
   local Hip-Hop culture 28
   male domination of
      Adelaide Hip Hop 96
   policing Australian Hip-Hop
      67
   radio station preference for
      'white' Hip-Hop 92
   rejection of commercialised
      American rap 63–4
   Thebarton Theatre
      performance 50–1
   vice-signaling 81
   'Walk On' and socio-political
      issues 55–6

J

Jupiter, Maya
   Australian Hip-Hop
      as marginalised
      counterculture 60

   challenges as female
      performer 97
   First Nations Hip-Hop 91
   Hip-Hop stories from diverse
      groups 98

K

'Karma' (1200 Techniques) 19
Kelly and Clapham
   'Decolonizing Aussie Hip
      Hop' (book chapter)
      14–15
   First Nations Hip-Hop 91
   local accents 15

L

Lal, Kish
   Hilltop Hoods as larrikins 56
   Hip-Hop and sexism 79
Lambert, Matthew (*See* Suffa)
larrikinism, meaning 56–7
Latukefu, Hau 95
Layla
   Australian accent in rap 18
   challenges as female
      performer 97
   contribution of Obese to
      Australian Hip-Hop 20
   launch of *The Calling* 47, 48
Lewps, Anthony
   battle raps 69
   contribution of Obese to
      Australian Hip-Hop 20–1

M

Madcap (aka Derek Dowling)
   70–1
male dominated culture 96, 97

Index

Maya (*See* Jupiter, Maya)
Midnight Oil 20
Mitchell, Tony
    criticism of Hilltop Hoods'
        lyrics 57
    Hip-Hop and non-Anglo
        Australians 14
Mitus
    defensiveness about
        Australian Hip-Hop 66
    Hip-Hop and religion 30
    misogyny and homophobia
        in *The Calling* 79–80
Murton, PJ
    Australian Hip-Hop
        as marginalised
        counterculture 59
    management of Hilltop
        Hoods 22
    Thebarton Theatre
        performance 50

N
Next, DJ 21
Noctis (book) 99

O
Obese Block Party 20
Obese Records
    album releases 17–18, 19,
        20
    contribution to Australian
        Hip-Hop 19, 20
    early history 17–18
    independent label 88
    mutual relationship with
        Hilltop Hoods 19

Out4Fame (magazine) 61
ozhiphop.com/forum 61–2

P
Pegz 17
'People in the Front Row'
    (Melanie) 40–1
Pollard, Mark
    flexibility in new Hip-Hop
        generation 100
    policing Australian Hip-Hop
        66–7
    socio-political issues in
        Hilltop Hoods' songs 55
posse tracks 69–70
Pressure 21
    Australian Hip-Hop
        development 22
    developments in Hilltop
        Hoods sound and style 89
    'Illusionary Lines' 58
    reactions to success of *The
        Calling* 87
    relationships with other Hip-
        Hop artists 66
    'Stopping All Stations' 57–8
    suspicion of major record
        labels 64
punchlines 36–7

Q
Quro 60–1

R
Raceless 16
racism among Hip-Hop fans 17,
    93–4

Index

122

Rakim 38
Ralph AL
    Australian Hip-Hop
        as marginalised
        counterculture 60
    recording of 'The Certificate'
        73
    role of Debris recording
        studio 73–4
    Thebarton Theatre
        performance 49
Rankine, Daniel (*See* Trials)
'Rattling the Keys to the Kingdom'
    (Hilltop Hoods) 94
Reclaim Australia 82
rhyme patterns 37–8
Rock, Thomas 93
Rose, Tricia, *Black Noise* (book)
    11–12

S

Safka, Melanie 40–1
Sanchez, DJ
    Hip-Hop as competitive 75
    increasing diversity and
        growth in Australian Hip-
        Hop 100
    launch of *The Calling* 47
    quality of *The Calling* 85
    white-dominated Hip-Hop 91
Saunders, Grant 15
sexism 77, 78, 79, 98
Shazlek One 17–18
'Show Business ft. Eamon'
    (Hilltop Hoods) 23
'Simmy and the Gravyspitter'
    (Hilltop Hoods) 80

Smith, Daniel (*See* Pressure)
'Speaking in Tongues' (Hilltop
    Hoods) 93
Staaf, Tirren (*See* Pegz)
Stealth (magazine) 61
'Stopping All Stations' (Hilltop
    Hoods) 57–8
Styles, Josie, DJ
    beat boxing 80
    friendships within Hip-Hop
        community 66
    increasing diversity in
        Australian Hip-Hop 94–5
    male-dominated culture 97
    performances by Hilltop
        Hoods 52
    support for women 97–8
Suffa 21
    collective political action 56
    Hilltop Hoods as 'break
        through' group 102
    Hip-Hop as Australian art
        form 13, 14
    Hip-Hop development in
        Adelaide 22
    Hip-Hop fans and racism
        93–4
    producing 'The Nosebleed
        Section' 40–1
    underground
        counterculture 87

T

'Testimonial Year' (Hilltop
    Hoods)
    commitment to Hip-Hop 26
    film clip 27

Index

123

as introduction to Hip-Hop
26
pride in local Hip-Hop
achievement 28
The Calling
contribution to Australian
Hip-Hop 19
key role changing Australian
Hip-Hop 101–2
launch 46–7
lyrics critiquing other groups
37
misogyny and homophobia
79–80
nostalgia for 101
promotion for launch 48
rhyme patterns 37
tours 51
types of tracks 42, 53
'The Calling' (Hilltop Hoods)
real vs fake Hip-Hop 30–1
religious themes 29, 31
The Calling Live (2005) (DVD)
49
'The Certificate' (Certified Wise)
battle raps 69
beat 72
recording of 73
vice-signaling 81
The Great Expanse 23
The Hard Road
success of 23
'What a Great Night' 82

'The Nosebleed Section' (Hilltop
Hoods)
accolades 39–40
film clip 51–2
meaning of name 41
for national anthem 40
production 40–1
'The Sentinel' (Hilltop Hoods)
19, 85–6
Tomahawk
Australian Hip-Hop
development 28
inclusion of 'Australian' in
describing Hip-Hop 16
MC battles 77, 78
Trials
Reclaim Australia 82
vice-signaling 81
triple j support for Hip-Hop
18, 39
Truth, Kaylah 99

V
Vito, Christopher 63

W
Waheed, Shaheen 17–18
'Walk On' (Hilltop Hoods) 55–6
'What a Great Night' (Hilltop
Hoods) 82
white Hip-Hop 17, 93–4, 95
Williams, Justin 12
Wire 15–16

Index